WATER IN CANADA

A RESOURCE IN CRISIS

Hanneke Brooymans

Foreword by Dr. David W. Schindler

CC
CANADIAN
CURRENTS

© 2011 by Canadian Currents
First printed in 2011 10 9 8 7 6 5 4 3 2 1
Printed in China

Distributed by:
Lone Pine Publishing
10145 – 81 Avenue
Edmonton, Alberta T6E 1W9

Website: www.lonepinepublishing.com

Library and Archives Canada Cataloguing in Publication

Brooymans, Hanneke, 1974-
        Water in Canada : a resource in crisis / Hanneke Brooymans.

Includes index.
ISBN 978-1-926736-04-4 (bound).--ISBN 978-1-926736-01-3 (pbk.)

        1. Fresh water--Canada. 2. Water-supply--Canada. 3. Water-supply--Government policy--Canada. 4. Water-supply--Canada--Management.
I. Title.

GB707.B76 2011   333.9100971   C2010-906657-X

Editorial Director: Nancy Foulds
Project Editor: Gary Whyte
Editorial: Gary Whyte, Sheila Quinlan, Wendy Pirk
Production Manager: Gene Longson
Designer: Gerry Dotto
Layout: Lisa Morley
Graphics Design: Gerry Dotto, Lisa Morley
Cover Design: Gerry Dotto
Cover Image: Peter Kirillov/Thinkstock (water in hourglass); Photodisc/Thinkstock (sand in hourglass); iStockphoto/Thinkstock (hourglass).
Back Cover Photography: Dina Trifonova/Hemera/Thinkstock.
Credits: All reasonable efforts have been expended to obtain permissions from respective copyright holders for graphics used in this book. The graphics are either in the public domain or are reproduced with the generous permission of the copyright holders. A full list of credits appears on pages 230–231, which constitutes an extension of this copyright page.
Author Photo: Ryan Jackson

We acknowledge the financial support of the Government of Canada through the Canada Book Fund (CBF) for our publishing activities.

PC: 19

Dedication

For Jul

Acknowledgements

Thank you to Ken Davis, of Lone Pine Publishing, for approaching me to write this book in the first place. I also appreciate all the hard work staff put into this book, especially that of Gary Whyte and Nancy Foulds, who I dealt with most.

David Schindler has been instrumental in the writing of this book in more ways than one. Not only did I learn some critical aquatics ecology lessons from him while attending the University of Alberta, he has also continued to share his expertise and unflinching commentary on all kinds of water-related issues with me through about 14 years of journalism now. That dates back to my days in college when he talked to me about pollutants in glaciers.

I thank all the scientists, activists, statisticians, politicians and business people out there who have delved into the water world and produced thought-provoking reports on those issues. Many of these folks took the time to speak with me and I appreciate that. I hope I've been able to do their work justice. They include: Maude Barlow, Nicole Biederbeck, Duncan Ellison, Richard Fernandes, Herb Gray, Steve Hrudey, Thomas Kierans, Robert T. Kristjanson, Al Kristofferson, Rob de Loë, Michael Miltenberger, Josée Miville-Dechêne, David Phillips, John Pomeroy, Frank Quinn, Bob Sandford, John Smol, John Sprague and Lorne Taylor. Apologies if I've forgotten anyone.

I appreciate that my managers at the Edmonton Journal allowed me to take a leave from work to write this book, not an easy thing for them to do during this time of restricted staff resources. My colleagues at the paper have all been very encouraging, which is really not surprising considering what a fantastic group of professional, hard-core journalists they happen to be. My home office lacked for only one thing—the daily inspiration they provide me. Special thanks go to Darcy Henton, whose sage advice gleaned from his own book-writing experience gave me invaluable insight and realistic expectations about the process.

Of course, I'd like to thank my parents, Corry and Jack, for their unstinting support and for cultivating in me an interest in all things outdoors from my early childhood.

And lastly, I am most grateful to my husband Jul, for being the rock I needed when I was drowning in my water work.

4

Contents

Foreword

CANADIANS TRADITIONALLY have taken freshwater for granted. We appear to be surrounded by water, and politicians and the media glibly and frequently reassure us that we have plentiful water supplies. Every day we hear of new industrial expansions, growing populations and housing developments, and it is simply assumed that water supplies will be adequate.

This cavalier view is uncomfortably at variance with what freshwater experts deal with and read about every day: lake levels and river flows are declining; wells are running dry or being polluted with arsenic or petrochemical residues; and lakes that were once blue and transparent are now undrinkable and unswimmable, with huge blooms of smelly and toxic blue-green algae. Meanwhile, the government agencies responsible for protecting water and the public interest have been the subject of relentless and successive budget cuts for decades. These problems are particularly acute in the west. As one expert exclaimed, "It is like the view from the locomotive 10 seconds before the train wreck."

Until now, understanding the many complicated interactions that determine the future of our freshwater has required years of study in disciplines ranging from hydrology and ecology to politics. Hanneke Brooymans has boiled down the many complications of freshwater science and governance into language understandable to all Canadians. She dispels the myth of water abundance and exposes what the cumulative effects of pollution, land use change, alien species introductions, climate change and the sheer numbers of humans are on our freshwater.

Hanneke also exposes the flaws in water governance that prevent us from solving these urgent water problems. Numerous federal, provincial and municipal agencies have separate, and often overlapping, responsibilities for water. The overlap actually hinders intelligent decision making, with bureaucrats spending more effort in "harmonizing" the efforts of agencies than on decision making. Vital decisions on water resources are often made by municipal governments using a single criterion: "Will it make us money?"

Finally, Hanneke discusses what we can and must do, at individual, municipal, provincial and national levels, to balance Canadian demand for water with our real, rather than mythical, water supply.

Water in Canada is written in the same clear and accurate prose that has characterized Hanneke's reporting for the *Edmonton Journal*. This book is an excellent and readable summary of a vast literature on Canadian water research and governance, exposing the many facets of one of the most urgent problems of the 21st century. It is a must-read for all Canadians concerned about the future of our water supplies and aquatic ecosystems.

—Dr. David Schindler

Killam Memorial Chair and Professor of Ecology
University of Alberta, Edmonton

Introduction

LATELY I'VE BEEN PONDERING how humans would handle environment issues if they lived to be 200 years old. How cavalier would people be about their tinkering with the atmosphere's carbon dioxide concentration, for example, if they knew they were the guinea pigs? And would the much longer life experience of our elders be of any benefit?

The past and future are weighing heavily on many management decisions in Canada today, but without a doubt one of the most critical areas will be the safeguarding of our water resources.

Canadians are not water rich—we only think we are. This delusion does not serve us well. Undoubtedly, we've been hypnotized by images of landscapes pockmarked with a multitude of lakes and laced with countless streams, creeks and rivers. The question that remains is: can we snap out of our collective delusion in time? Maybe. But that would require a significant boost in the country's collective water literacy, which is currently as shallow and murky as a mud puddle.

A 2010 poll revealed that one-quarter of us have no idea what the original source of tap water is in our homes. So it's doubtful that many of us would know that almost all of the water in Canada is fossil water—a geological gift left behind by retreating glaciers after the last ice age. The actual renewable water that lands on Canada in the course of a year as rain or snow represents seven percent of the planet's quota, which is surprisingly proportional to the almost seven percent of land surface we occupy. That amount still seems like a generous serving for a population that represents just half of a percent of the world's human population, but more than half of that water makes a beeline north, far away from where the vast majority of us are hunkered down in the south. Most of it flows to the Arctic Ocean or to Hudson Bay.

The water that we do have to work with faces increasing pressures. In 1867, our fledgling country held 3.4 million Canadians. As of April 1, 2010, there were already 10 times that many. Agriculture and industry have grown, too. And we have learned to harness our fortunes to energy production, which requires a vast amount of water whether it be nuclear or coal-fired power plants or the long, convoluted process that winnows gasoline out of oilsands. So while we might have started out with a cappuccino-cup–sized thirst, we've more than graduated to the full-fledged Big Gulp®.

And there, looming in the hazy distance is the prospect of Mother Nature's climate change hangover. Just how thirsty she's going to be remains an open question. It depends on how hot the planet is going to get, and since humanity has made very little effort to keep climate change to a minimum, she's likely going to be parched.

Canada's northerly position means the temperature change will be much greater than the global average increase; the further north you go, the greater the difference will be. Climatologists have already cast a worried eye to the Canadian Prairies, where water tends to be naturally less abundant than in other areas of the country. Parts of the Prairies have just undergone the driest back-to-back years our rain gauges have ever measured. And each of the last 10 years in some areas was drier than normal, a very unusual trend. While this drought is extremely worrisome for farmers, there is evidence that the climate has meted out much longer and more severe droughts even when not under the influence of climate change. It is frightening to imagine what might happen with that added factor in the mix.

This is where a longer-lived ancestor might come in handy. Surely they would have warned us not to spend to the edge of our water limits—like we've done in some parts of the Prairies and interior British Columbia—during a period of relative abundance, knowing the superfluous supply could at any time be snatched away.

Climate modelers are also suggesting that nature may begin delivering water to us much more erratically. There could be very little water for a long time and then, like a distant candy-dispensing aunt who rarely visits, there could be a sudden, overly generous serving that makes us sick. Violent storms, of the one-in-a-hundred-years variety, have already clobbered cities like Toronto and Edmonton, causing millions of dollars in damage. Climatologists uncomfortably note that these supposedly rare storms are becoming far too common.

Aside from dealing with water quantity issues, we're also going to have to watch water quality. Pollution is a problem that could really bite us in the pocket book if we're not careful, warns Bob Sandford, an Alberta-based water expert. If we don't make efforts to keep pollutants out, we can expect problems with water to occupy more and more of our time and concern, he says. "And we can also consider that what water is telling us is going to end up with surprising and very expensive impacts in domains that we can only anticipate now which will affect all of our economic sectors and limit our social and economic development in the future."

Yes, humans are an adaptable species. But do we want our grandchildren drawing on shrunken, polluted streams and rivers and frolicking in filthy puddles that used to be crystal-clear lakes and thinking this is normal?

It could easily happen. People think the natural environment they encounter during childhood is the norm, and they measure any additional environmental degradation against that yardstick. Peter Kahn, a human development psychologist, calls this environmental generational amnesia. "With each ensuing generation the amount of environmental degradation increases, but each generation in its youth takes that degraded condition as the non-degraded condition—as the normal experience."

The problem grows with each passing year as more of the population grows up urban and less in touch with wilderness. At Confederation, the proportion was 80 percent rural, 20 percent urban. Now it's the opposite. So while the science sharpens on exactly how much water our natural ecosystems need to thrive, Canadians are increasingly out of touch with the benefits of giving nature the water it needs.

We are at a crossroads. Will we decide to live comfortably within our still-evolving natural limits? Or will we make life difficult for ourselves and everything around us?

PART ONE

Quantification and Health of Our Water Supply

FAT DAFFODIL BUDS AT THE beginning of February are nothing but a daydream in most of Canada, but they're reality in John Sprague's yard on Salt Spring Island. The daffodils time their growth spurt perfectly. They've just lapped up a three-month flush of rain. Sprague knows they're not going to get much more throughout the year. The island receives about two-thirds of its rain from November to January, he says. And it's not all that much. The rest of the year is so dry that "You don't touch your lawn from about May to October," Sprague says.

The island is only 14 kilometres wide, so just about all of the island's 10,500 residents see an abundance of water all around them almost every day. And yet, freshwater is scarce. Or, more accurately, the population is pushing against the limits of the supply. "There is a water shortage on this little island because we're living on a rock and there's not much water in the ground," Sprague says. "A lot of people depend on the water they collect from their roofs." That's what they use to water their gardens throughout the drier months, he says.

Sprague, a retired aquatics biologist, is not unfamiliar with the concept of water scarcity. He's been exasperated for decades now about this misconception Canadians have about the superabundance of their water supply, but he's not surprised that many Canadians are under this spell. "It's because you look around and you see all these lakes and it looks like a lot of water." That's deceptive, though, he says. In reality, you can only depend on what's replenishing them every year, what's falling from the sky. Not knowing the difference is dangerous. "Mostly the attitude that we're blessed with this wonderful abundant supply of water, it just leads to a profligate attitude, a wasteful attitude."

Sprague has been on a one-man public education campaign on this subject. He's been writing letters to the editor since 1985, he says, stamping out any notion of superfluous supplies. And in 2007 he wrote a chapter on the myth of water abundance in a book called *Eau Canada: The Future of Canada's Water*. "Canada appears to have a lot of water," he wrote, "but this is because of a topography that creates a few large lakes and many shallow, small lakes along with a cool climate and low evaporation of the water."

On Salt Spring Island, where the population has expanded from 450 in 1895 to over 10,000 today, the story of what could happen in other parts of Canada is already unfolding. "There's a big water war going on here about how much you can supply, how much development can go on, and how many subdivisions you can supply. It's an argument that has been raging for several years."

CHAPTER ONE

Quantification of Our Water Supply

WHERE DOES THE WATER that we do get come from, and how much is there? Unless you're one of the 1 billion people worldwide living without clean drinking water or perhaps one of the 2.6 billion lacking adequate sanitation, chances are you don't think much about the source of the water running from your tap.

Freshwater is actually relatively rare. Although Planet Earth is awash in water, about 97 percent of that is in the salty oceans. Of the 3 percent that is not saline, 99 percent is either locked up in icebergs and glaciers, or is tucked out of sight underground. A measly 0.0002 percent of all water on earth is found in rivers, and that's what the majority of human beings rely on for their water supply. Freshwater lakes contain another 0.008 percent.

Distribution of Earth's Water

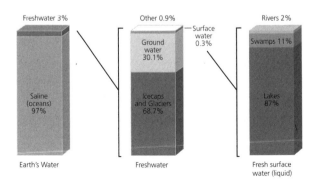

For those who want to go back even further and question how the earth came to have water, there are thought to have been a multitude of sources. Astronomers think planetesimals, bodies thought to be orbiting the sun during the time planets were forming, carried ice and water. Ice and water vapour were swirling around in the atmosphere when the earth formed. And some of what was in the earth's interior has been transferred by volcanoes to the atmosphere. Even more water was added from comets.

How Much of Earth's Water is Available for Our Use

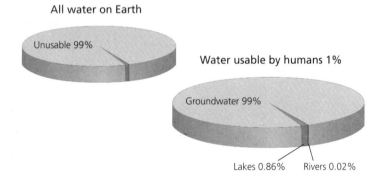

Mechanics: the Hydrologic Cycle
=================================

The transportation system responsible for moving all of this water around is called the hydrologic cycle. It's the endless loop by which water falls to the ground, eventually evaporates, travels through the atmosphere and then falls back to earth.

The main cog in the hydrologic cycle is arguably the heating of the ocean's surface by the sun. A vast amount of freshwater is lifted up out of the ocean. This is possible because energy from the sun's rays allows individual water molecules to escape the strong bond that ties them to neighbouring water molecules. The molecules rise up into the atmosphere as vapour—this process is known as evaporation.

The higher they go, the cooler they get and soon the water molecules condense on dust particles. If it's really cold, they will condense into ice, snow or hail. Otherwise, they become a liquid again. The water particles collect together into clouds and sail across the sky, driven by air currents. As they move around, they collide and merge with more water particles driven into their midst by updrafts. When the droplets become too heavy to hang in the air, they fall as rain. (Incidentally, raindrops are not tear-shaped. High-speed cameras reveal raindrops resemble the top of a small hamburger bun, flattened on the bottom and dome-shaped on top.) If the surrounding air is cold enough—as it often is in Canada—it will fall as hail or snow.

When the moisture falls in a frozen form, the cycle temporarily stalls. Until the temperature increases enough to allow melting, most of the moisture is stored as ice or snow. Only the process of sublimation can convert some of the ice or snow directly into water vapour. If the precipitation falls as rain, its fate will depend on how thirsty the ground is. A parched landscape will normally soak up every molecule of water it can get. That water, in turn, can get taken up by the roots of a plant, which may emit the water again as vapour in a process called transpiration. If the rain falls on a sated, waterlogged landscape with a slope, the water will be forced to move on. This runoff flows to low points in topography, known to us as creeks, streams, rivers, ponds and lakes.

If the water is allowed to collect and sit, it can percolate downward through the soil and rock layers. What may look like solid ground to us is actually a combination of sand and gravel, large rocks, and even blocks of limestone. Each of these materials has cracks, crannies and pores that water will slide into. The porosity, or volume of pores, determines if the material will hold the water or if it will slip through. Sand, for example, is famous for big, well-connected pores and therefore good drainage. If the material is very permeable like sand, the water could move several metres in a day. But when water hits clay or shale, movement can be miniscule, creeping along at rates as low as a few centimetres in a century.

Ultimately, as long as the water can squeeze into an open, unfilled passage below it, it will continue to travel downward. When a water molecule hits a spot where the ground below it is already saturated, it has reached the water table. Everything below the water table is officially groundwater. A zone of rock or other porous material that can hold significant amounts of groundwater qualifies as an aquifer. Water that makes its way down to these aquifers is recharging them.

Aquifers are infinitely various: they can sit close to the surface or dwell thousands of metres down. They can be replenished relatively quickly or can be closed-off systems, created many millennia ago and then sealed off by geological events. These so-called fossil aquifers can be massive. The largest, the Nubian Sandstone Aquifer, underlies four African countries.

Confined aquifers: these exist where the groundwater is bounded between layers of less permeable substances like clay or dense rock. These are also called **artesian aquifers.** When a well is drilled into this kind of aquifer, the water rises above the level of the aquifer because of the confining pressure.

Unconfined aquifers: as the name implies, this aquifer is not bounded by impermeable layers of rock or clay. Instead, its upper boundary is the water table. These aquifers are usually near the surface and so are easily recharged—and also easily contaminated.

Fractured aquifers: water in these aquifers travels through cracks and fractures in otherwise solid rock, such as granite. Groundwater in limestone aquifers can carve out larger openings, such as channels and caverns.

Groundwater in aquifers is often clean and potable, partly because it's naturally filtered as it moves through the ground. But the water may also be tainted with naturally occurring arsenic or salts. It can also be poisoned by human carelessness or ignorance. This contamination often happens at the head of a groundwater well, where harmful substances can enter if the well casing (the tubular lining of a well) is not maintained or protected.

Groundwater is an important contributor to water levels in streams, lakes, rivers, marshes and oceans. Most of us don't know how vital the connection is because we can't see this process, called discharge, happening. One form of visible discharge greatly valued by landowners is a spring, which occurs when the water table intersects with the land surface.

How Much Water Does Canada Really Have?

A misconception about Canada's water supply has led to some serious oversights. Mostly, we've been pretty lax about keeping tabs on how much we have and what's been happening to that supply. The general but misleading impression of abundance is perhaps the reason why few attempts have been made in the past to measure Canada's assets of renewable freshwater, wrote François Soulard and Mark Henry, Statistics Canada employees in the environment division, in a 2009 report. That's right—2009. Why would we hurry to measure something we think we'll never run out of, right?

The past attempts that were made to measure our renewable water resources weren't done in a consistent manner, Soulard and Henry note. Unfortunately, this lack of consistency means we can't compare the results over time and space. And yet, those results are exactly the kind of information that is necessary to manage water resources adequately, they warn. "This is especially true in a context where water resources are affected by competing uses and changes in the climate."

Resource managers of all stripes believe this basic truth: you can't manage what you don't measure. Not knowing what the trends are is a major handicap. But the environment division at Statistics Canada intends to change and make more consistent measurements now.

How Much is Contained in Lakes and Rivers?

There's not a whole heck of a lot of solid information to start with, though. "Lake volume data in Canada is not generally available," Soulard wrote in a paper produced for an audience of environmental accountants meeting in Rome in 2003. While water held in lakes is measured for a few of the larger lakes (80, to be exact), volume for the remaining 2 million smaller lakes remains unknown. These lakes are, however, relatively shallow, and most likely do not contribute much when compared, for example, to Lake Superior, or the 645 other lakes that are larger than 100 square kilometres. Based on the relationship between the area and the volume of the lakes for which volumes are known quantities, Soulard estimated these 645 lakes would hold 17,398 cubic kilometres of water.

The Largest Canadian Lakes and the Volume of Water They Hold

Largest Canadian Lakes			
Lake	Volume (when available)	Area	Portion in Canada
Lake Superior (Ontario)	12,100 km³	82,100 km² (total)	28,748 km² (Canada)
Lake Huron (Ontario)	3540 km³	59,600 km² (total)	36,000 km² (Canada)
Great Bear Lake (NWT)	2236 km³	31,328 km²	
Great Slave Lake (NWT)	2088 km³	28,568 km²	
Lake Erie (Ontario)	484 km³	25,700 km² (total)	12,768 km² (Canada)
Lake Winnipeg (Manitoba)	N/A	24,387 km²	
Lake Ontario (Ontario)	1640 km³	18,960 km² (total)	10,334 km² (Canada)
Lake Athabasca (Alberta/ Saskatchewan)	N/A	7935 km²	
Reindeer Lake (Saskatchewan/ Manitoba)	N/A	6650 km²	
Nettilling Lake (Nunavut)	N/A	5542 km²	
Lake Winnipegosis (Manitoba)	N/A	5374 km²	
Lake Nipigon (Ontario)	N/A	4848 km²	
Lake Manitoba (Manitoba)	284 km³	4624 km²	
Lake of the Woods (Ontario)	N/A	3150 km²	
Dubawnt (Nunavut)	N/A	3833 km²	

It's also unlikely that Canada will ever measure the volume of all its rivers, given the geographical scope of the country and the complexity of its hydrological network—there are more than 8500 named rivers in Canada, and countless other un-named rivers and streams, he said.

Longest Rivers in Canada
(over 1000 km in total length)

The river lengths cited below are measurements from the farthest source to the ultimate outflow. In some cases, this means a river changes names several times along its route (thus, for length purposes, the Mackenzie River includes the Slave, Peace and Finlay rivers). The table lists the components proceding upriver. To avoid double-counting, component parts are not listed separately even though both the Peace River and South Saskatchewan rivers are at least 1000 km long.

Longest Rivers in Canada				
Rank	Name (at outflow)	Length (km)	Outflow	Component Parts
1	Mackenzie	4241	Beaufort Sea	Mackenzie - Slave - Peace - Findlay
2	Yukon	3185 (1143 km in Canada)	Bering Sea	Yukon
3	St. Lawrence	3058 (small part wholly in United States)	Gulf of St. Lawrence	St. Lawrence - Niagara - Detroit - St. Clair - St. Marys - St. Louis
4	Nelson	2575	Hudson Bay	Nelson - Saskatchewan - South Saskatchewan - Bow
5	Columbia	2000 (801 km in Canada)	Pacific Ocean	Columbia
6	Churchill	1609	Hudson Bay	Churchill [of Manitoba and Saskatchewan]
7	Fraser	1370	Pacific Ocean	Fraser
8	North Saskatchewan	1287	Saskatchewan River	North Saskatchewan
9	Ottawa	1271	St. Lawrence River	Ottawa
10	Athabasca	1231	Slave River	Athabasca
11	Liard	1115	Mackenzie River	Liard
12	Assiniboine	1070	Red River (part of the Nelson River drainage basin)	Assiniboine

Maximum Discharge of Rivers in Canada

The data are the mean annual discharge at the furthest downstream gauging station within Canada. The data are net of diversions (that is, they include diversions into the river basin and deduct flow diverted out of the particular river basin). Discharge data are in cubic metres per second.

Maximum Discharge of Rivers in Canada			
Rank	Name (at mouth)	Maximum Discharge (m^3 per second)	Outflow and Notes
1	St. Lawrence	9850	Gulf of St. Lawrence
2	Mackenzie	9700	Beaufort Sea
3	Fraser	3540	Pacific Ocean
4	La Grande	3359	James Bay
5	Nelson	3130	Hudson Bay
6	Columbia	2790	Pacific Ocean
7	Yukon	2300	Bering Sea
8	Koksoak	2010	Ungava Bay
9	Churchill [of Newfoundland and Labrador]	1914	Labrador Sea
10	Moose	1370	James Bay

How Much is Renewable?

Like Sprague, Soulard cautions that water shouldn't be thought of as inexhaustible. "Water is often described as a renewable resource," he writes. "This is only partly true. For example, although the Great Lakes (including the United States' portion) contain 23,000 cubic kilometres of water, 98 percent of this amount is 'fossil' water, left over from the last ice age." What we really need to pay attention to is how much water we have under the "renewable" category.

Soulard and Henry did their best to quantify two basic components of these renewable water assets: groundwater that flows back to the surface; and rain and melted snow that flows over the ground and eventually reaches a surface waterbody, called runoff.

Once all the runoff numbers were collected, this is what they came up with: the national estimate of the volume of water runoff is calculated to be, on average, 3470 cubic kilometres per year. This number sounds vaguely massive, but largely meaningless. Soulard and Henry obligingly put this number in perspective: experts estimate that, worldwide, irrigation consumes 2664 cubic kilometres of water each year, they wrote in their report. Or, as another example, Lake Huron contains 3540 cubic kilometres of water.

The smugness is flooding back, isn't it? There's more: that water yield works out to approximately 100,000 cubic metres per person, they calculate. That's 100 million litres each. And even though Canadians are astonishingly inefficient water users—more on that later—each person uses about 120,000 litres a year. The Canadian economy, Soulard and Henry say, withdraws only about 1.4 percent of this volume annually, most of that being used and then discharged back into the same watershed it was pulled from.

How Much is Available?

But hold on. Soulard and Henry go on to turn the spigot on that cask of confidence. "These national figures do not capture two important dimensions: the location and the timing of the withdrawals, and the location and the timing of the availability of water resources."

In other words, it makes no sense to be collectively smug. Canada is too vast a country for that, with differing climates and water supplies. We also tend to use our water for different things depending on where we live. The federal water survey folks also note that approximately 60 percent of the country's freshwater drains to the north, away from the vast majority of the population that lives within 300 kilometres of our southern border.

Ocean Drainage Areas and Drainage Regions of Canada

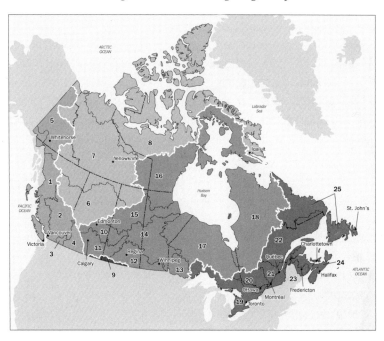

Pacific Ocean
1   Pacific Coastal
2   Fraser-Lower Mainland
3   Okanagan-Similkameen
4   Columbia
5   Yukon

Arctic Ocean
6   Peace-Athabasca
7   Lower Mackenzie
8   Arctic Coast-Islands

Gulf of Mexico
9   Missouri

Hudson Bay
10 North Saskatchewan
11 South Saskatchewan
12 Assiniboine-Red
13 Winnipeg

14 Lower Saskatchewan-Nelson
15 Churchill
16 Keewatin-Southern Baffin Island
17 Northern Ontario
18 Northern Québec

Atlantic Ocean
19 Great Lakes
20 Ottawa
21 St. Lawrence
22 North Shore-Gaspé
23 Saint John-St. Croix
24 Maritime Coastal
25 Newfoundland-Labrador

 Ocean drainage
area boundary

Shown here are 5 ocean drainage areas and 25 drainage regions of Canada.

Soulard and Henry looked at a first attempt that was made to map the relationship between the availability and demand for water in Canada. They saw that water used by the Canadian economy could represent more than 40 percent of the water flows in some areas of the country, on an average annual basis. "For instance, the water intake to streamflow ratio reached 43 percent in the South Saskatchewan, Missouri and Assiniboine–Red drainage region. Water intake was also a high proportion of streamflow in the North Saskatchewan drainage region and in the Great Lakes/St. Lawrence drainage region."

What we need to do, they say, is study the availability of Canada's renewable water assets on a regional basis, for specific time periods. In his 2003 paper, Soulard averaged net precipitation per capita per sub-basin, and then weighted this average by the share of its population. "The result of this formula indicates that Canada does not have over 100,000 cubic metres of (net) precipitation per capita, but rather 450 cubic metres," he wrote. "Instead of ranking amongst the leaders in terms of water renewal per capita, Canada ranks 165th amongst nations."

In this sense, Canada's collective water confidence quickly melts down as some areas, each with their own unique circumstances, struggle within the confines of tight water supplies. Part of the struggle comes from the incredible variability in the amount of precipitation each region receives. Annual precipitation ranges from 50 millimetres in the far north to as much as 4000 millimetres on the Pacific Coast, according to the federal Water Survey Branch.

As Soulard and Henry point out, certain parts of the country experience more variability than others in the amount of precipitation they receive annually. The Prairie Provinces and parts of central and southeastern British Columbia represent the areas of highest variability, they note. They plan to study this variability in more detail. It's important to figure out how it fits in, given changing, and often competing, demands for water resources.

There is more up-and-down news on Canada's water supply. An estimated 12 percent of Canada is covered by lakes and rivers, according to Statistics Canada. This sounds great. But while many provinces have a substantial amount of water in comparison with their population, only 3 percent of the area covered by water in Canada is located in inhabited regions, the agency says. This unevenness means that Ontario, with 39 percent of the population, has 8.8 percent of the water area, while the Northwest Territories and Nunavut, with just 0.2 percent of the population, have 43 percent of the country's water area, the agency notes. The Great Lakes are not counted since they are interjurisdictional.

Measuring What We Have, As Best We Can

"You can't manage what you don't measure." Again, this old saying could not be more true for anything than for water. How would farmers figure out how much livestock they could raise without knowing how much water they will be able to access? How could a city water utility manage its water treatment plant without knowing how much it could count on to flow down the river it pulls water from?

Canadians cottoned on to this notion of measuring water more than a century ago. Residents of Alberta and Saskatchewan began quantifying their surface water supplies in 1894, before those districts were even formally declared provinces. That was the year the Dominion of Canada passed the North West Irrigation Act. The government allocated water to farmers, and so it had to know details about the water source.

Monitoring Surface Water

Today, a nationally coordinated system collects and distributes all kinds of water data. The Water Survey of Canada, the federal agency responsible for this work, traces its roots back to 1908, when the country decided it needed a formal approach to pin down the extent of the nation's water resources.

The program has been continuously operated, in general, by the federal government, except in Québec, where the province took over the responsibility in 1963. More than 100 years after the Water Survey first sprang up, the need for its work is increasingly important, the agency says. "As pressures on our water increase, the need for reliable hydrologic data and information becomes more urgent. The data collected by Environment Canada and its partners make it possible to manage this vital resource and the environment that it nourishes."

In 2010, there were 2859 active stations on lakes, rivers and streams of many sizes, according to the Water Survey branch. Costs are shared among federal, provincial and territorial governments. About half of the active stations transmit data in near-real time. An additional 5595 hydrometric stations are no longer active, but their data are stored in a national database.

The federal government has faced considerable criticism for reducing the number of monitoring stations. John Pomeroy, the Canada Research Chair in Water Resource and Climate Change, says the stream gauge network has been declining in many countries over the last few decades, but especially in Canada. "In fact we stand out," he says. "At one point our decline in stream gauge coverage in the north was equaled only by the former Soviet Union, which had a far better excuse for its decline in stream gauges because it broke up." Pomeroy says monitoring took a very serious hit in the 1990s, when the federal deficit was brought back in line.

Monitoring agencies do the best they can, with sharing of duties and information going on between the provincial and federal governments. Some wealthier provinces such as Alberta were able to fill in the decline in federal expenditures and even advance beyond what the federal government had done, but places like Saskatchewan and the Northwest Territories were not able to, Pomeroy says. Even in Alberta, monitoring is taking a hit as the provincial government struggles with declining revenues from the hard-hit oil industry.

Those thousands of stations are needed, though, because there is a dizzying array of ecosystems, each with a different water makeup, scattered across Canada's vast landscape. "Water and environmental issues are directly related to the hydrologic and socioeconomic conditions of each region," the agency says. "The management of those issues therefore requires an understanding of the regional hydrology."

Not only that, but measurements are also the only reliable indicator of the status and trends of the available surface water across the country and as such are essential for making decisions that concern water, the agency adds.

The agency knows its system has limitations. Most of its stations are in the southern half of the country, where the population and economic pressures are greatest. This was a wise thing to do, but it also means our knowledge about waterbodies in the north is much weaker, something the agency readily admits.

Mapping Groundwater

Even more worrisome, many scientists would say, is our lack of knowledge about our groundwater supplies. There is far more water underground than on the surface. Groundwater includes any water that exists underground, whether that be in channels or more commonly in the spaces between particles of soil or in the crevices and cracks in rock. An estimated 8.5 million Canadians, or 26 percent, rely on groundwater as a drinking water source, according to Statistics Canada figures from 2007.

Yet although groundwater has been routinely surveyed since the early 20th century, it has not been mapped in a systematic way, the department says. Around 2002, the department began a concerted groundwater mapping program to correct this oversight.

The program manager, Alfonso Rivera, is quite passionate about the matter. In an online newsletter he wrote:

> I was recently asked several questions: Why is it important to know our groundwater resources now? Why is it important to conduct a national inventory of our groundwater resources? What issues are affecting the inventory? What issues would emerge without that inventory? Why do we care about knowledge gaps?

> Those questions appalled me. The short, quick and easy answer to all those questions: to know! As scientists, we tend to do research for the sake of knowing (as with early scientists, such as Aristotle and Socrates). But in today's society, knowledge provides more than our need for scientists' self-esteem. Knowledge has become the backbone of development, of well-being, of productivity. Knowledge has become the basis for decision-making processes.

Rivera says he often receives requests for groundwater knowledge from ordinary Canadians, such as Gulf Islands residents, Alberta farmers and Ottawa citizens. They ask him, "Should we expect saltwater intrusion into our wells? Are the oil industries going to dry our aquifers? Is my well going to be affected by my neighbour?" And he answers, "I still cannot answer such questions. I am surprised that in this highly industrialized country, we still do not know our groundwater resources."

Ultimately, a national groundwater inventory will reduce costs in supplying water to users, reduce risks of overexploitation and contamination, and resolve land use conflicts, according to Natural Resources Canada. Rivera hopes to publish a book on Canada's groundwater resources by the end of 2010.

In the meantime, an expert panel from the Canadian Council of Academies released a study in 2009 that said a more rapid pace of aquifer mapping is needed. "The last comprehensive assessment of Canada's groundwater resources was published in 1967," said the government-commissioned report. "The Groundwater Mapping Program managed by the Geological Survey of Canada has undertaken to assess 30 key regional aquifers. At current rates, it is expected the mapping will not be complete for almost another two decades."

That's not fast enough to collect the information required for better groundwater management, the panel noted. For example, in Alberta's Athabasca oilsands, it is not known if the area can sustain the groundwater demands and losses given the development predicted for the region. Generally speaking, there isn't even enough information to draw the boundaries of what would be considered the source water protection zones for aquifers.

The panel also stressed the need to catch up with emerging contamination issues. "Little is known about the transport and fate in the subsurface environment of new forms of contamination that may be present in treated sewage effluent, e.g., pharmaceuticals and personal-care products," it wrote. "This knowledge gap should be filled. Resources allocated to such threats to groundwater quality have not kept pace with needs."

It also pointed to the need to keep up with human-caused contamination from agriculture, contaminated sites or leaking storage tanks and sewer systems. "These sources need to be identified, remediated where possible, and inventoried in provincial databases, and advisories need to be provided to groundwater users," said the panel.

CHAPTER TWO

Health of Our Water Supply

WHEN IT COMES TO THE safety of their water supply, Canadians' confidence has declined slightly in the last few years, from 81 percent in 2008 to 79 percent in 2010, according to an Ipsos Reid survey that is done annually on water attitudes. They view pollution as one of the biggest threats to our freshwater supply. Run-off pollutants from land to water were chosen by 19 percent of those surveyed in 2009 as the biggest threat. Another 12 percent chose illegal dumping of toxins. Both of these factors can seriously affect water quality. But so can mismanagement of water by municipal, provincial and federal governments, chosen by another 12 percent. Global warming and climate change (8 percent) and mass export of water to the U.S. (17 percent) were also seen as threats.

When Canada's population was smaller, there were rural and urban practices we could get away with—our rivers and lakes could absorb the impacts—but these habits become ever more damaging as the population swells. And our growth shows no signs of slowing down: between 2001 and 2007, the country added 2 million people. Among the G8 nations, we had the fastest growth between 2001 to 2006, when our population rose 5.2 percent, according to Statistics Canada.

It's true that if you divide these numbers across a vast territory of nearly 10 million square kilometres you get a low population density: about 3.5 people per square kilometre. But that's not an accurate way of representing our ecological population pressure. While the north is lightly populated, the south sees concentrations of up to 238 inhabitants per square kilometre in some of the census metropolitan areas, Stats Canada says. What we all do, individually and collectively, has an enormous impact on our water.

Pollution and Nutrient Overload

Currently, humans pollute the water around them in two general ways. The first is more easily dealt with, and that's point source pollution. The second is harder to grapple with, and that's non-point source pollution.

The Ontario Ministry of the Environment defines point source pollution and non-point source pollution as follows:

Point source pollution enters the water system at a specific place from an identifiable source. This type includes industrial discharges, oil and chemical spills, wastewater discharges from municipal sewage treatment plants and septic systems and leaking storage tanks.

Non-point source pollution is caused when rain or snow runs over land and picks up natural and manmade pollutants before entering a body of water or an aquifer. Examples include agricultural runoff (manure, pesticides and fertilizers) and urban runoff from streets and sidewalks (oil, salt, pesticides, pet droppings, chemicals, litter).

Sewage and Wastewater

Canada's federal government tracks the pollutants emitted by the biggest point sources, whether they be industrial, commercial or other facilities. They are required to report their pollutant emissions each year. This information is published online by the National Pollutant Release Inventory (NPRI). Their most recent detailed report available showed that 122,201 tonnes of pollutants were released to waterbodies in Canada in 2008. The vast majority of that amount—86 percent—was from water and sewage systems. This sector includes municipal sewage treatment facilities that receive and treat much of the large amount of wastewater produced by households, businesses and industries. Wastewater contains numerous pollutants, but most of it consists of nitrate ions, ammonia and phosphorus. The 2009 data shows that two of these three pollutants had increased from the year before. Only ammonia had dipped slightly. Wastewater can also contain certain toxic metals such as zinc, copper, mercury and cadmium. The federal government estimates Canada's wastewater systems release 6 trillion litres of wastewater effluent each year.

Releases To Water
(reported to the NPRI for 2008, by Industrial Sector)

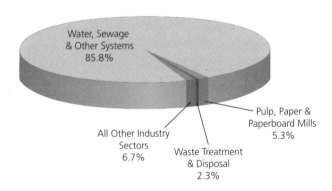

In February 2010 the federal government finally announced that it will be enacting new regulations that set standards for the discharge from all wastewater facilities in Canada. There will now be national standards limiting the amount of suspended solids, chlorine, ammonia and biochemical oxygen demand in the effluent coming out of wastewater treatment plants. "Today we are taking action to protect our environment for future generations," said the Environment Minister Jim Prentice at the time of the announcement. "It is not acceptable that we continue discharging untreated waste into our waterways." The goal is to protect human and environmental health as well as fish populations from the contaminants in wastewater.

The government acknowledged that municipal wastewater effluent is one of the largest sources of pollution to Canadian waters. It said that this new Canada-wide Strategy for the Management of Municipal Wastewater Effluent was endorsed by the Canadian Council of Ministers of the Environment (CCME) in February 2009 to better protect Canadians and their environment. Releasing raw sewage into our waterways will no longer be permitted, the government says.

If releasing raw sewage sounds like a shocking notion in this day and age, keep in mind that a whole bunch of communities on Vancouver Island, including the province's capital, Victoria, still dump their untreated sewage into the Strait of Juan de Fuca. In 2006 the province's environment minister ordered them to stop this practice. He had received a report that said the two outfall sites were so filthy they warranted preliminary contaminated site designation. Since then, the region has been struggling to figure out how it's going to handle the 129 million litres of liquid waste it generates daily. Normally, the waste is disposed of after only a simple screening that removes "plastics, paper, vegetative matter, and organic lumps," according to a report prepared by a scientific and technical review panel.

A plan to deal more thoroughly with the sewage, which will involve several treatment plants, was delivered to the province at the end of 2009. If everything goes smoothly, one or more of the decentralized plants is expected to be in operation by early 2013, with other facilities, including a biosolids management facility, in operation by the end of 2016, according to the organization handling the project.

To their credit, the communities are talking about next generation waste treatment. They're looking at extracting heat for use in buildings, generating biomethane to reduce reliance on natural gas, using dried sludge as a fuel for cement kilns, and reusing effluent for irrigation and toilet flushing.

On the country's other coast, people seemed to have the same philosophy of dilution being the solution to their sewage. Halifax's sewage treatment plant didn't come online until 2008. Then, in January 2009, heavy rain and a mechanical malfunction shut the plant down. It was down for more than a year, allowing sewage to flow into the city's harbour, just like before. In June 2010 the plant was finally operational again.

Of course, coastal communities are not the only ones releasing wastewater of questionable quality into our rivers, lakes and streams. Cities across the country dump sewage—sometimes untreated, sometimes partially treated—into waterbodies through bypasses or combined sewer overflows.

A bypass happens when a wastewater treatment plant receives too much sewage. If the sewage backs up, basements could flood, so the sewage is redirected and discharged into the local waterbody with little or no treatment. A deliberate decision to bypass the plant could also be taken if the plant is undergoing a maintenance shutdown.

Combined sewers are the legacy of an earlier era when pipes were built to carry both sewage and storm water. During wet weather, these pipes carry a larger volume of wastewater than treatment plants can handle, and they overflow from outfalls into nearby rivers. In Edmonton, where about 20 percent of neighbourhoods had combined sewer systems, it was estimated that complete sewer separation would cost about $2.5 billion. The city is slowly separating some of the combined sewers when they are doing other neighbourhood renewal work. It also built 19 storage tanks with a capacity of 25 million litres to reduce the amount of overflow entering the river. Other cities grappling with the issue include Toronto, Winnipeg, Montreal and Vancouver, to name a few.

In 2009, Ecojustice wrote a report about the sewage dumped into the Great Lakes and Ontario's waterways each year. The Ontario Ministry of the Environment estimated that the total volume of sewage dumped from sewage treatment plant bypasses was approximately 18 billion litres in 2006 and 8 billion litres in 2007, with at least seven municipalities releasing more than a billion litres each in 2006–2007, the organization wrote. That amount doesn't cover the total volume coming from bypasses, though, because the province does not collect data for 215 sewage treatment facilities that are operated by the Ontario Clean Water Agency (OCWA), one of the province's own agencies, the report added. The picture is even murkier on combined sewer overflows because the volume and frequency of the overflows are not routinely measured, estimated or consistently reported.

Ecojustice pointed out that it is not overtly illegal to dump sewage via a bypass or overflow under Ontario law, particularly if it is done during wet weather to alleviate high flow volumes. "There are provincial government guidelines in place that municipalities can follow, however the guidelines are not enforceable and merely encourage but do not require reductions in sewage dumping." The environmental group recommends money be spent on sewage systems to increase capacity and improve treatment. Without this increased investment, sewage dumping through combined sewer overflows and bypasses is likely to increase as climate change causes increased wet weather and storm events in Ontario, Ecojustice predicts.

The new federal regulations on wastewater require that overflows not increase in frequency and that "floatables" be removed. The government expects it could take up to 30 years and between $10 billion and $13 billion for the new wastewater standards to be implemented at all of the country's 3700-plus wastewater facilities. The majority of the wastewater system costs would be borne by municipalities, as they own and operate the vast majority of the wastewater systems in Canada, says the proposed legislation. But the federal government has several programs that earmark wastewater as a priority, so some money will come from them.

Spending will be spread out over the 30 years because the plan is to pay for needed upgrades on a risk basis. Risk will be judged by first measuring what each wastewater plant currently spews into the environment after treatment and then by checking how sensitive the receiving environment is to that effluent. The plan is for high-risk facilities to meet the national standards first, followed by medium- and low-risk facilities. To make the rules stick, Environment Canada proposed new regulations under the Fisheries Act. The budgeted amount doesn't include costs for managing combined sewer overflows.

Once the regulations come into effect, a minimum of secondary treatment will be required. The coastal areas and Quebec will need the most upgrades. Three of the Atlantic provinces and Quebec have less than 50 percent of their population served by sanitary sewer systems with secondary treatment or better, the proposed regulations say. British Columbia has approximately 36 percent of its served population receiving less than secondary treatment.

Duncan Ellison, executive director of the Canadian Water and Wastewater Association, expects the standards will be met before the time frame. "This comes down to the big city, small city issue. Most of the big cities are already meeting or are below the levels, so it will not be a problem for them." But Ellison said the association believes the $13 billion allocated to bring everyone up to standard will probably not be enough. "And it only deals with the raw capital. It doesn't include the added operating costs that would go along with it."

Phosphorus and Eutrophication

One of the biggest problems with sewage has always been the fact that it's loaded with phosphorus. This element is an essential nutrient for plant growth. Early in his career, aquatics ecologist David Schindler became convinced that phosphorus was a key in the rapidly deteriorating condition of the Great Lakes. Lake Erie and Lake Ontario were both murky with the masses of algae that thrived on overabundant nutrients. This process of overfertilization and the resulting reaction is called eutrophication.

In a lake, the algae in the upper layer of water are called phytoplankton, and it's these organisms that have caused and could continue to cause great problems for humans and wildlife in the 20th and 21st centuries. "Phosphorus and nitrogen, the two elements that most commonly limit plant growth in lakes, are 1000 times more concentrated in sewage effluent than in the waters of lakes unaffected by humans," Schindler and John Vallentyne wrote in their book *The Algal Bowl: The Overfertilization of the World's Freshwaters and Estuaries.* "Therefore, it is not surprising that their addition to natural water has an effect like turning up the volume control of an amplifier, in terms of accelerating the growth of plants."

In 1968, Vallentyne hired Schindler as part of the team he put together to study eutrophication. A year later, Schindler began the first of the experiments that are now famous in the annals of aquatics research. The research took place at the Experimental Lakes Area in northwestern Ontario, midway between Kenora and Dryden. These lakes, now 58 in number, are designated by the federal and Ontario governments as research watersheds and are operated by Fisheries and Oceans Canada.

By controlling the levels of nutrients in these small lakes, Schindler and his colleagues were able to show that it was indeed phosphorus that caused rampant algal blooms, and not some other element, as the detergent industry tried to claim. One of the most convincing arguments was a picture that showed the hourglass shape of one of the experimental lakes split in two by a sturdy nylon curtain. Nitrogen and carbon were added to both halves, but phosphorus only to one. The half of the lake that had not received additional phosphorus was clear. The other half had huge algal blooms. By this time Canadian regulators were already convinced of the link, but the picture was used many times in hearings on eutrophication control, which were held on a state-by-state basis in the U.S., say Schindler and Vallentyne in their book.

Since then, phosphorus has been limited to low concentrations in sewage effluent, particularly from wastewater treatment plants on the Great Lakes. "In the Great Lakes, what we were able to do is to declare victory over the point sources," recalls Schindler as he sits in his University of Alberta office, a blue winter sky visible through the tall rectangular window in his eighth-floor office. "There were only two of any significance. One was detergents and the other was municipal sewage effluents." Those two sources were about half the problem, and tackling it back in the 1970s seemed to offer enough of a solution to satisfy most people. Politicians relaxed.

Schindler continued to conduct research at the lakes until the late 1980s, including research on acid rain's effects. But he soon grew tired of the constant fight for funding, and when the University of Alberta offered both him and his wife academic positions, he made the move. Two years later, he was awarded the Stockholm Water Prize in 1991, the equivalent of a Nobel Prize in the water science world, for his body of work.

But Schindler and Vallentyne knew all this time that point sources were only half the problem. And as they note in their book, unfortunately, the contribution from other sources has increased in the past 30 years. Vallentyne died shortly before *The Algal Bowl* was published in 2008. It was actually his second edition—he'd written the first *Algal Bowl* solo in 1974. But Schindler speaks for both of them when he says eutrophication is still a huge problem. "Globally, that's probably the most important water quality problem of all. It's happening everywhere there are people. Lakes are turning green all over. Of course Alberta's no exception. We've got all these little basins of green slime that people buy million-dollar cottages on, which I've never been able to figure out."

In the 21st century, the problem stems more from agriculture, as fertilizer use and livestock culture have increased, the duo wrote. "Runoff of nutrients from paved streets, roads and mismanaged urban and rural lands also adds nutrients to our freshwaters. These so-called 'non-point sources' of nutrients are much more difficult to control than the makeup of detergents or the point-source effluents from sewage treatment plants."

Schindler and Vallentyne have focused a lot of their attention on the increasing "urbanization" of livestock into dense concentrations on feedlots. Much of the meat from this type of production is destined for foreign markets, but the manure remains a domestic problem. And these animals are much more prolific poop producers than humans. "In Alberta, an average beef cow produces 11 times more phosphorus in waste per day than a human. A medium sized pig produces 10 times more than a human. In other words, a 30,000 head CAFO [confined animal feeding operation] for cattle produces as much phosphorus as a city of 330,000 people!"

In 2009, there were 5.87 million head of cattle in Alberta and 1.5 million pigs. Given the same ratios of phosphorus production used in *The Algal Bowl*, that works out to almost 48,000 tonnes of phosphorus, equivalent to what almost 80 million humans would produce. And that's in a province of about 3.6 million people. Granted, not all of this ends up in waterbodies, but even a small fraction of that amount in local waterbodies can cause problems. In comparison, the wastewater treatment plants for Edmonton, Calgary and Red Deer, which handle the sewage produced by the bulk of the province's population, released 172 tonnes of phosphorus in 2008, the most recent figures available. Actually, all of

Canada's wastewater treatment sector released 4925 tonnes in 2008.

All of the nutrients in the animal waste initially come to the hog farms and feedlots as food for the livestock. Whether it's corn or silage, the vast amounts required often means that food is imported from another area, and what would often be another watershed. But wastes from these factory farms are not usually returned to those areas because their high water content makes them heavy and costly to transport, Schindler and Vallentyne say.

They explain that even if the manure is carefully applied to croplands, the plants cannot take up all of the phosphorus. The excess phosphorus bonds to soil particles. Wind or water can sweep this nutrient-rich soil into lakes or rivers. The problems are compounded by people stripping out wetlands, those precious "kidneys" of the ecosystem, which clean up and filter water as it runs through them.

There are ways to keep this manure from reaching waterways, of course. In Ontario, the Grand River Conservation Authority runs a rural water quality program that gives money to farmers who want to improve water quality. They can get grants to pay for ways to keep cattle out of waterways, prevent erosion by planting trees, and build proper manure storage facilities. Over 123 kilometres of stream had been fenced by the end of 2009 to restrict over 10,500 head of livestock from watercourses, keeping 71,000 kilograms of phosphorus on the land, the authority says.

Human behaviour around the sensitive riparian edges of lakes and streams can make things worse, too. Schindler says municipalities in Alberta now realize septic tanks are a bad thing, and they're willing to require people to put in pump outs. "They don't realize that about half of the nutrient input is from what people do with messing up the lake shore," he adds. "They strip out all the trees. There's erosion when they build the cabin. They let their pets run loose. They fertilize their flower gardens and their lawns."

On July 1, 2010, the federal government further tightened the noose on phosphorus when its latest regulation came into effect. This tightening was in response to concerns expressed by Canadians about the proliferation of harmful algal blooms in the country's lakes and rivers, the government said. The new rules, which actually amend an existing regulation, say that algal blooms and over-fertilization are serious issues in numerous areas, including Lake Simcoe in Ontario; Lake Winnipeg in Manitoba; the Bow River in Alberta; the Qu'Appelle River system in Saskatchewan; the Okanagan basin in British Columbia; and other waterbodies in Prince Edward Island and Quebec. The new regulation lowered the allowable concentration of phosphorus in laundry detergent and introduced a concentration limit to hand dishwashing soap, automatic dishwashing detergent and household cleaners. The government expected the regulation to reduce the release of phosphorus into the environment by an estimated 28,400 tonnes over 25 years.

But in some areas the changes are too late, and the resulting algal blooms have damaging effects. People living near the blooms may moan about the unsightliness and the stench, but some blooms can exact a much more permanent toll. Toxins are released by what we commonly call blue-green algae. These organisms, which are not actually algae, are more properly named cyanobacteria. They've been around for about 3.5 billion years and are credited with generating much of the oxygen in our atmosphere today, but as fabulous as that accomplishment might be, these bacteria are now a danger to any terrestrial animal that might want a sip of water from a bloom-infested lake.

Health Canada says about 50 to 75 percent of blooms are capable of producing toxins, and often more than one toxin is present in these blooms. The department has known this for quite a while and points to one study done in Alberta between 1990 and 1992 in which more than 70 percent of over 380 bloom biomass samples from 19 lakes showed detectable levels of toxin. The toxic effects of cyanobacteria on livestock have been recognized for more than 100 years, it adds.

The toxins produced by cyanobacteria have a range of effects. Some target the liver (hepatotoxins), while others can devastate the nervous system (neurotoxins). Others may merely irritate the skin. Health Canada has set a guideline for microcystin, the most common toxin. Although humans are not likely to try to drink untreated, stinky algae-infested water, those who think they can purge the danger by boiling the water are wrong—the toxins will persist. It's just a good idea to avoid water with blue-green algae altogether, especially for children and pets.

Health authorities have issued advisories warning people about the toxins from as geographically diverse areas as Lake Utopia in New Brunswick to Lesser Slave Lake in Alberta.

The Case of Lake Winnipeg

Lake Winnipeg suffers from toxic blooms, too. Very high concentrations of microcystin have occasionally been detected during intensive off-shore algal blooms and along shorelines during bloom events, according to Brian Kotak and colleagues who work with the Lake Winnipeg Research Consortium. The concentrations were at times over 2000 micrograms per litre, while the World Health Organization drinking water guideline is one microgram per litre.

The lake has been plagued with horrendous algal blooms since 1992. That was the year Robert T. Kristjanson noticed something had gone terribly awry. "We went to George's Island that spring," recalls Kristjanson from his home in Gimli, Manitoba. "We set our nets, we couldn't even hardly get them up." Even the large motorized lifters in the big boats could barely pull the nets up. "They were so full of algae. It was just like a wall. *That* was the start of it."

Kristjanson comes from a long line of fishers. His Icelandic grandfather began fishing on the lake in 1891 and the family has been in the fishing industry ever since, a span of 118 years. "We are four family generations of fishing captains," says Kristjanson, 76, who sails the *Lady Roberta*, a 60-footer named after his daughter. His son and grandson are in the business, too. "There are three generations of us right now that are fishing side by side. There's been nothing easy about it, but fishing is our business."

And Kristjanson has not been shy about speaking up to protect his livelihood. He called a television crew down to the lake for a look. There was a lot of media coverage, and calling attention to the problem turned out to be simple.

But solving it has turned out to be complicated. The core issue is the already familiar blight of eutrophication. Al Kristofferson was a federal fisheries biologist living in the area at the time Kristjanson called the camera crews out to the lake. "I grew up in the same town as this fellow lives in, that's Gimli on the shore of Lake Winnipeg." He remembers looking at the broadcast and saying, "Wait a second, this is something that I recognize. I understand it. I think we've got an issue here. And so did a number of other federal government people whom I happened to work with."

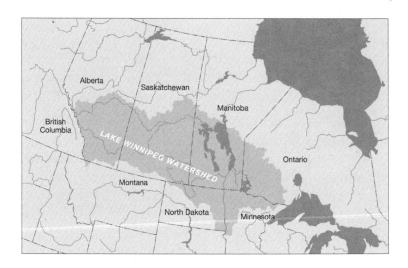

They decided to investigate, and it didn't take them long to realize what was causing the trouble. "What's been happening over time, and nobody has been deliberately doing it, but…we've little by little been contributing more nutrients to the system than were naturally there before," says Kristofferson, now the managing director of the Lake Winnipeg Research Consortium.

The consortium was created in 1998 to coordinate scientific research on the lake. When the research crew headed out onto the lake in August 1999 aboard a former Coast Guard ship called the *Namao*, they encountered an algae bloom that stretched for 160 kilometres continuously, Kristofferson says. "There was the visible evidence of a serious issue developing in the lake." Further investigations clearly show that the current concentrations of nitrogen and phosphorus in Lake Winnipeg far exceed those that existed historically, he says.

As to where the nutrients are coming from, well, that's the answer that will make this a rather thorny problem to solve. Lake Winnipeg is the penultimate stop for water draining a massive watershed of 1 million square kilometres that stretches from the Rockies in the west almost to Lake Superior. Ultimately, the water flows to the Arctic Ocean. About 6.6 million people live within the lake's massive watershed. Most of them—about 5.5 million people—live on the Canadian side of the border. Another 1.1 million people reside on the U.S. side. The excess nutrients flowing into Lake Winnipeg come from throughout this watershed. "So the issue is certainly an international issue, a cross-border issue, and an interprovincial issue," Kristofferson says.

Even though the lake is the 10th largest freshwater lake in the world, it cannot resist the cumulative nutrient pressures it faces. "We've used satellite monitoring of the lake to keep an eye on the extent of these blooms and the persistence of these blooms, and we know it's because of human activity. The situation seems similar to when Lake Erie suffered its eutrophication problems in the late '60s and early '70s," Kristofferson says. "At that time, they weren't sure the process was reversible," he adds. "Some thought Lake Erie was finished."

But a lot of work was done to get a clear understanding of the nature of the problem, and once that was accomplished, people began to do things differently at the insistence of government and the science community. After about 12 or 14 years of reducing their nutrient inputs to the watershed, they found there was a significant improvement in water quality. But there are important differences in the two stories. "The Lake Erie watershed is really small, and most of the input was coming from point sources, large sewage systems," says Kristofferson. True, they spent billions turning the situation around. "But the challenge we have is very different because we have literally millions of non-point sources, even in Edmonton and Calgary and the far-flung reaches of the watershed."

Kristofferson says they don't know yet how much phosphate and nitrogen is making the difference between what the lake received historically versus now. "We're working on that, actually. The way we can go back in time is to take cores of the sediments of Lake Winnipeg. That's being done as we speak."

The Lake Winnipeg Stewardship Board said in a 2006 report that Lake Winnipeg receives about 8000 tonnes of phosphate from the major river systems each year, and that a good portion of that is coming in via the Red River, even though the Red provides only about 11 percent of the water by volume. "A huge portion of the phosphate getting into Lake Winnipeg is coming in via the Red River, and a little more than half that is coming from south of the border," Kristofferson sums up.

Kristjanson says there have always been algae blooms in the lake. "But what you would notice is that in a bay in the fall, it would come in there. But it was a skim on the water. It wasn't down 40 feet [12 metres]."

He remembers his reaction to what happened in 1992. "You were really mad. Where does this stuff come from?" When the television crews came out, he asked, "What are we going to do? We didn't make this."

Kristjanson has literally relied on the lake since birth for sustenance, both as a means of financial support for his family and for drinking water. "When I wanted a drink of water I just walked out to the dock, picked a pail of water, walked home, put it inside the kettle. That was what you drank. I'm still here."

Although Kristofferson can say that contaminants are not a problem and fish in the lake remain safe to eat, he doesn't have good news about the lake's overall condition yet. "The situation in Lake Winnipeg isn't getting any better," he says. "In fact, it's gotten worse since we started looking at it. So we haven't even slowed the speeding train down yet. We've got to slow it down and then we have to reverse it."

The first thing they have to do is make everybody aware of the fact that they have to, as best as they possibly can, reduce their contributions to these loadings by understanding what's going on and looking at the sort of things they're doing, he explains. "People in cities for instance, there are all these...guys who go roaring around fertilizing your lawn for you. Well maybe you shouldn't do that." Pet excrement is an issue as well, he notes. There have been studies that showed that pet excrement can add up to a huge contribution when it's run off in stormwater systems during rain events.

Kristofferson says the research consortium isn't into assigning responsibility for the problem. "The business of laying the blame is absolutely ridiculous. Everybody, myself included, yourself included, is contributing to a greater or lesser extent in this whole thing. We've had this finger-pointing issue going on for the longest time and it's still going on. The agricultural people are blaming the city people, the city people are blaming them. That's just a waste of time. If you want to point the finger, point it at yourself and say, what is it that I'm doing? That's the sort of attitude that has to prevail if we're going to turn this around."

In February 2003, more than 10 years after Kristjanson first called attention to the issue, the Manitoba government unveiled a provincial action plan to protect Lake Winnipeg. One of the six points in the Lake Winnipeg Action Plan was the establishment of the Lake Winnipeg Stewardship Board. The board's role is to help the province implement its action plan and most importantly to identify actions necessary to reduce nitrogen and phosphorus loading to Lake Winnipeg to pre-1970 levels.

In 2005, the board gave the government directions in 32 areas that would help solve the problem. Those recommendations were further refined in December 2006. One of the things the board did in the recommendations report was define where the nutrients were coming from, as best as they could. Close to half of the phosphorus appears to be coming from within Manitoba, while the other 53 percent is from the U.S., Saskatchewan, Alberta and Ontario, according to the board's report.

In 2009, the board delivered a report on how well the government has implemented the recommendations. The report also included an update on progress by non-provincial agencies toward achieving the recommendations. Kristjanson, who is on the board, was impatient for the government to release the report to the public. When it came out in March 2010, the report rated progress by the province on 79 of the 135 individual recommendations (59 percent) as satisfactory. Another 9 (6.5 percent) achieved an excellent grade, while 38 (28 percent) were marginal and 9 (6.5 percent) were unsatisfactory.

One of the recommendations was that the province should continue to require that nutrient reductions be implemented as quickly as possible in the larger Manitoba cities. In its progress report, the board said the province needs to make a concerted effort to complete its nutrient management strategy and develop ecologically relevant nutrient objectives for Lake Winnipeg. Also, more effort is needed to recycle nutrients in wastewater effluent and to reduce nutrient loading from urban stormwater and agricultural land drainage.

Nutrient removal technologies are in place in other large prairie cities that discharge to the Lake Winnipeg watershed such as Edmonton, Calgary, Saskatoon and Regina, the board had pointed out earlier. These cities are currently required to meet phosphorus limits of 1 milligram per litre and 5 to 15 milligrams per litre of nitrogen. Once Winnipeg falls into line, the total nutrient load to Lake Winnipeg will be reduced by approximately 2.5 percent.

But the city battled the province over demands that it reduce nitrogen concentrations in its wastewater. It insisted that, in keeping with the best scientific advice it has received, phosphorus removal is key to improving conditions in Lake Winnipeg, where the treated water flows, but nitrogen removal is not beneficial. And it said that removing the nitrogen would require upgrades that would cost $350 million in capital costs alone, plus another $194 million in debt financing costs, and $9 million in additional annual operating costs.

The city even brought in David Schindler to make its point before a joint city-province meeting. "There's not a case history anywhere in the world to show that it works," said Schindler, prior to that meeting, about the removal of both phosphorus and nitrogen. "And there's a lot of evidence that suggests the more you cut back on nitrogen the more blue-green blooms you're going to get because it favours species that can fix nitrogen. So they could spend more money and even see the problem worsen as a result."

It's not the first bit of animosity stirred up by this battle against algae. Kristjanson said both he and Kristofferson have been "raked over the coals" for their efforts by people who say "we're going to ruin the lake and ruin this and ruin that."

Everyone from pig farmers to the City of Winnipeg have had their hackles up, fearing they would face an unfair burden in the overall struggle to lessen nutrient flows to the lake. Kristjanson says it comes down to everyone doing the right thing. "You can't keep on dumping this on the land endlessly. We are taking a little parcel of southern Manitoba here and polluting tens of thousands of miles right to the ocean. Do we have that right? Do you have that right and do I have that right? Because we say we're making money."

He says he's reminded of how environmentalists are attacking Alberta's oilsands operators and government for the production of "dirty" oil. "Let's put it into perspective then. I'm calling (this) dirty water. I don't want your dirty water. And that's not personal."

Kristjanson says the phosphorus problem is something everyone in the basin has to work together to solve. "It is something we have to sit down and decide on as Canadians what we can do. We're not half-wits. This was all done in our era."

Drinking Water Quality: the Numbers

A critical starting point in ensuring good drinking water quality is taking care of the source water. Source water can be surface water in rivers, lakes or even in dugouts in rural areas. It can also mean groundwater. This source water makes up the raw water that we then treat, whether it be in a large municipal treatment plant or by using a reverse osmosis system in your house. Keeping the source clean obviously makes it much easier to provide safe drinking water. If there are less bacteria or chemical contaminants in the water to begin with, there are less to remove.

The federal government keeps an eye on the quality of surface freshwater, not only for source protection reasons, but also to make sure the water is clean enough to support aquatic life, such as fish and invertebrates. In any case, quality of aquatic life is a reflection of how well the water is being protected from pollutants and overuse.

Environment Canada says water quality is under pressure from a range of sources, including wastewaters from urban and suburban development, runoff from agricultural fields, effluents from industrial facilities, acid rain and household behaviour. Tests done at 379 monitoring sites, including 11 lake sites and 368 river sites in southern Canada, rated water quality as excellent at 24 sites (6 percent), good at 159 sites (42 percent), fair at 113 sites (30 percent), marginal at 68 sites (18 percent) and poor at 15 sites (4 percent), the department says.

Measurements of freshwater quality in 2006 for the Great Lakes were calculated using 2004 and 2005 monitoring data. Freshwater quality was rated as good or excellent for Lake Superior, Lake Huron, Georgian Bay and eastern Lake Erie, fair for central Lake Erie, and marginal for western Lake Erie and Lake Ontario.

Environment Canada says no long-term trends are available for this national indicator. Water quality monitoring data from across Canada were assembled nationally for the first time in 2005 and covered the 2001–2003 period. At least 10 years of data are required to present reliable trends, and reporting on the index has not yet covered a sufficient time period. Although no long-term trends are available, a comparison of the results from the 2006, 2007 and 2008 Canadian Environmental Sustainability Indicators revealed only minor changes during this period.

On a worldwide basis, Canada is thought to be doing well in its water care-taking duties. The Environmental Performance Index is a long-standing scorecard created by Yale and Columbia Universities. Among the 10 categories it looks at are water resources for human health (access to drinking water and sanitation) and water resources for ecosystems (water quality and scarcity indices and water stress). It also looks at agricultural water intensity. If Canada was ranked solely on these factors it would be at the top of the class. In 2010 it earned 100 percent in the water resources for human health category, and 90.7 percent for ecosystem water resources. Its agriculture grade was 89.5 percent. Predictably, Canada got clobbered in the climate change category, with a 37 percent grade that brought its average down to 66.4 percent and a 46th place finish. When ranked among the Americas,

Canada sits in a very modest middling spot, 14th out of the table of 28, handily thrashed by first-place Costa Rica.

Drinking Water Quality: the Reality

A more practical perspective on Canada's water quality comes from Canadians themselves. Unfortunately, despite the glowing international grades, there are plenty of people dealing with dreadful water quality.

The Safe Drinking Water Foundation, based in Saskatoon, was incorporated in 1998 by five scientists from Canada, Russia, Scotland and Japan. The scientists shared a concern about the plight of rural people who lacked access to clean drinking water, said Nicole Biederbeck, the foundation's education director. "In a lot of rural communities water quality isn't as good as it is in urban communities," she says. "They don't have as many resources... [The founders] were going to help people in developing countries, but they found out we have lots of problems in our own backyard in Canada, especially in First Nations communities."

Inadequate Drinking Water Systems for First Nations

If there is one Canadian group that suffers an unfair burden of unfit drinking water, it is the country's First Nations. These communities and the federal government have grappled with this problem for decades, to no apparent resolution.

Indian and Northern Affairs Canada found a significant risk to the quality or safety of drinking water in three-quarters of the drinking water systems they assessed in First Nations communities in 2001, says the most recent report on the issue by the Commissioner of the Environment and Sustainable Development. The issue is an urgent one, especially since the on-reserve population is expected to grow by 230,000 between 2004 and 2021. In 2003, the government made drinking water safety in First Nations communities a priority and approved a budget of $600 million over five years for the First Nations Water Management Strategy, the 2005 report says.

As of December 31, 2009, there were 112 First Nations communities across Canada under a drinking water advisory. Given that the number of communities stands around 600, that means about 15 percent of First Nations communities don't have drinkable tap water. The majority of advisories weren't one or two day inconveniences, either. Between 1995 and 2007, a total of 162 advisories had been in effect for longer than one year, according to a Health Canada report published in 2009. Dozens of communities have had advisories in effect for multiple years—one as long as 13 years. The most common reasons for the advisories were inadequate disinfection, unacceptable microbiological quality and equipment malfunction.

The federal government began a First Nations water management strategy in 2003, and at first it seemed to make things worse. The number of communities under drinking water advisories shot up by over 50 percent. That increase is partly because unresolved long-term advisories were carried over from previous years and because more problems were likely being found as the number of water samples tested increased seven-fold between 2002 and 2006, according to Health Canada.

One of the worst situations played out in Kashechewan, Ontario. In 2005, the Cree First Nation town had 970 of its 1700 residents evacuated for medical treatment following concerns about water quality. Massive amounts of bottled water were flown into the community, along with a military water purification system and certified water treatment plant operators. The government also sent in people to repair the water treatment plant.

A federal representative who looked into issues and possible relocation options for the community in 2006 found that inadequacies and operational deficiencies had existed for some time at the water treatment plant and that since the contamination and subsequent flood events, great sums of money have been expended to resolve them. A single eight-hour shift, five days a week, was replaced with 24/7 operations. Pumps were replaced, chemicals are now being added by automated instrumentation, water pressure and quality are now being monitored by instruments, proper records are being maintained, and Class 2 Operators (employees of Northern Water Works, from Red Lake, Ontario) are now on duty 24 hours a day. At the time of the investigation, local operators had not yet been properly trained or certified.

Having inadequately trained operators is a common problem on reserves, as it is in many non-reserve rural communities. The 2005 commissioner's report noted that as of March 2005, 40 percent of operators on reserves were certified.

In 2006, the federal government announced another plan of action for safe drinking water in First Nations communities. That commitment amounted to $60 million over two years. In 2008, they threw another $330 million over two years onto the pile. And most recently, in 2009, the government pegged $165 million to go toward building or upgrading 18 water and wastewater infrastructure projects on reserves.

Is all of this money making a difference? The most recent progress report of April 2009 said the number of high-risk drinking water systems had been reduced from 85 to 48. Only four of the 21 priority communities identified in March 2006 remain on that list, and the number of water treatment operators with their first level of certification or greater has increased from 41 percent to 64 percent.

Duncan Ellison, executive director of the Canadian Water and Wastewater Association, says one solution to this issue, which is common in rural areas, is centralizing water treatment into a relatively big plant and then piping the treated water out to a number of small communities, which would maintain their own distribution systems but not have to produce the water. Not only would such a system ease the difficulty of finding enough competent operators, but it also turns out to be cheaper.

The per capita cost of the infrastructure has significant economies of scale, Ellison says. So a small town would probably have to spend $10 million on a treatment plant for 6000 people which gives you a very high capital cost, while a large city would probably only have to spend 30 times that amount for a population that is 100 times greater.

Until the department of Indian and Northern Affairs solves the widespread drinking water issue, conflicts and concerns will continue to flare up. And aboriginal communities are becoming increasingly outspoken about their drinking water worries. The community of Fort Chipewyan, Alberta, blames recent cases of rare cancers on contamination of the Athabasca River by upstream oilsands companies. A community physician, Dr. John O'Connor, reported his suspicions about rare cancer cases to the provincial health authorities and to the general public.

The Alberta Cancer Board eventually did a detailed study of the cancer cases in the community and found 51 cancers in 47 people in Fort Chipewyan, compared to 39 cancers expected. The study found higher rates of blood and lymphatic cancers and soft-tissue cancers, of which two cases were found. Three cases of bile-tract cancers were also found, two of which were a specific type called cholangiocarcinoma, a rare liver cancer. The head of the board said at the time that the extra cases could be due to chance but that health officials should carefully track cancer cases in the community over the next 5 to 10 years. The local people are convinced the water is the cause, though, and have pushed the provincial government to do more intensive research on the health of the people and the surrounding environment.

Their fears are fueled by fresh research by a team of scientists, led by Erin Kelly and David Schindler at the University of Alberta. In 2009 and 2010, they published research that showed that oilsands development was increasing the amount of toxic polycyclic aromatic compounds and heavy metals in the Athabasca River watershed.

Together with Fort Chipewyan residents, the scientists also showcased a collection of deformed fish that they had pulled from the river, as well as from Lake Athabasca and the Peace-Athabasca Delta. The fish are increasingly being found with tumours, lesions and deformities, the local fishers said. They called for the federal government to study fish health in the watershed.

Further attention was called to the situation when film director James Cameron decided to visit the oilsands and Fort Chipewyan to assess the situation himself. The director of Avatar said he found himself increasingly drawn to the environmental struggles faced by indigenous peoples around the world. He called Alberta's oilsands a gift to the country that could become a curse if not managed properly.

In British Columbia, the Okanagan Indian Band blockaded Tolko's entrance to the Browns Creek watershed in early 2010. The band wanted to prevent logging within the watershed that supplies them with much of their drinking water. They were worried the logging would sully their water supply. "The federal government has done nothing to protect the 1800 people who live on the Okanagan Indian Band reserve," said Chief Alexis at the beginning of the blockade. "The provincial government has made it clear that the financial interests of Tolko are of greater concern to them than the health and safety of the people who derive their drinking and irrigation water from the Browns Creek watershed."

The founder and long-time executive director of the Safe Drinking Water Foundation was keenly aware of the inadequacy of many drinking water systems on First Nations reserves. Hans Peterson was approached by an environmental health officer in 1999 about the situation on the Yellow Quill reserve in Saskatchewan. The community had been under a boil water advisory since 1995, and people were getting sick. The health officer had tried calling every agency connected with water, with no response. Peterson was soon heavily involved in creating a water treatment system that would work for the community. He lived at Yellow Quill from 2002 to 2004 developing the system, said Nicole Biederbeck, the foundation's education director. The $7 million facility opened in 2004, but tragically burned down in early 2010.

Water Mismanagement in Walkerton and North Battleford

By the 21st century, and with all our economic and scientific advantages, it seems we should have conquered the task of ensuring safe, clean drinking water for all of us. But fresh into the new millennium we soon learned that was not the case. Canadians are all too familiar with two of our most famous cases of water mismanagement: Walkerton and North Battleford.

The first was in the town of Walkerton, Ontario, in May 2000. Seven people died and 2300 of the 4800 residents became ill after the municipal water supply was contaminated with *E. coli* and another bacteria called *Campylobacter jejuni*. Justice Dennis O'Connor, who headed the inquiry into the calamity, found that the primary source of contamination was manure spread on a farm near one of the wells from which the town drew its water. The farmer who spread the manure was following the rules, but there were shortcomings in the monitoring of the well, in the provincial inspections programs and in operator training.

And perhaps most fatally, the people on whom the citizens of Walkerton relied to provide them with clean water could not be counted on. "For years, the [Public Utilities Commission] operators engaged in a host of improper operating practices, including failing to use adequate doses of chlorine, failing to monitor chlorine residuals daily, making false entries about residuals in daily operating records, and misstating the locations at which microbiological samples were taken," O'Connor wrote in his inquiry report.

If only the townsfolk had not had to rely on a well with so many chinks in its armor. Justice O'Connor noted there were likely direct pathways, such as fence post holes and a reversing spring, through which the contamination travelled from the surface to the bedrock and the aquifer. It also didn't help that the well was a shallow one, with the casing extending only 5 metres below the surface. The water from the well was drawn from an area of highly fractured bedrock. This fracturing, and the geological nature of the surrounding bedrock, made it possible for surface bacteria to quickly enter into fractured rock channels and proceed directly to the well, O'Connor concluded. "Raw water contamination by coliforms and fecal coliforms was indicated in the initial pump tests in 1978 and continued to May 2000." With such a consistent pattern of contamination it should have been clear that careful, constant treatment was needed.

The lesson learned by Walkerton residents on behalf of all Canadians has been a long, bitter one. For some residents, the experience has left a lasting physical affliction. In 2010, a team of scientists from McGill and McMaster universities published research that showed that 36 percent of the people who became ill also developed a type of post-infectious irritable bowel syndrome. "These patients suffer from chronic abdominal pain, discomfort, bloating and disturbed defecation...," said John K. Marshall, one of the principal investigators. It's an unpleasant way to live the remainder of your life.

About a year after the needless deaths and illnesses in Walkerton, in March and April of 2001, North Battleford, Saskatchewan, experienced an outbreak of gastrointestinal illness. A Health Canada study found that between 5800 and 7100 people in the area had fallen ill. In this case it was the parasite *Cryptosporidium parvum* that caused the havoc. The bug was in the North Saskatchewan River, the source of the town's drinking water. Had the town followed what's called the multi-barrier approach to its full extent, the bug could have been neutralized. But Justice Robert Laing, who ran the inquiry into the North Battleford incident, found this was not the case.

The multi-barrier approach includes source water protection—in other words, trying to make sure the bug and other contaminants don't get into the river in the first place. The second component involves water treatment, which means cleaning the water so it's fit to drink. And the last part is the design, construction and upgrading of the system used to distribute the clean water.

Recognizing the Importance of Source Water Protection

Both Laing and O'Connor stressed the importance of source water protection. "A strong source protection program offers a wide variety of benefits," O'Connor wrote. "It lowers risk cost-effectively, because keeping contaminants out of drinking water sources is an efficient way of keeping them out of drinking water. This is particularly so because some contaminants are not effectively removed by using standard treatment methods. As a result, protecting drinking water sources can in some instances be less expensive than treating contaminated water. Moreover, protecting sources is the only type of protection available to some consumers—at present, many rural residents drink untreated groundwater from wells. The protection of those groundwater sources is the only barrier in their drinking water systems." That's a pretty convincing list of reasons for treating water sources with respect, but source protection rarely happens with the thoroughness required.

Now it's true that drinking water can contain many naturally occurring elements and bacteria that would be there without human activity, but there is no doubt that we humans are adept at making things much worse than they have to be. North Battleford, for example, had the added handicap of having its drinking water intake downstream of the outflow of its wastewater treatment plant.

But it's not as if the town had a pristine source to begin with. North Battleford has the misfortune of depending on a river that first runs through the width of Alberta, a province that ranks number one in the nation in its cattle inventory. Alberta Agriculture and Rural Development estimated there were 5.87 million head in 2009. There were also 1.5 million pigs. "Livestock have been shown to be a significant source of *Giardia lamblia* and *Cryptosporidium parvum*," Laing wrote in his report. "Due to relatively long winters in Alberta and Saskatchewan, a significant reservoir of *Giardia lamblia* and *Cryptosporidium parvum* can be stored on the land over the winter and has the potential to be washed into the river during spring melt."

Edmonton's drinking water supplier, Epcor, has to deal with this problem constantly. Stephen Stanley, the general manager of operations for Epcor Water Services, testified at the inquiry that especially in spring, the level of oocysts, the thick-walled spore of *Cryptosporidium*, "are high compared to anywhere in North America on the North Saskatchewan River." The same year that Laing released his inquiry report, Epcor installed what was then the world's largest ultraviolet disinfection system. UV light is one of the few effective methods known to knock out *Cryptosporidium*. It deactivates their DNA structure, which in turn means they can't multiply.

In the Walkerton and North Battleford cases, the cause of human illnesses was animal waste tainting water, followed by inadequate treatment. So why not prevent the water from being contaminated in the first place? "It makes little sense that we go to great lengths to remove pathogens and nutrients from human sewage by expensive treatment, but little or no treatment is given to the far greater proportion of wastes from livestock," wrote aquatics ecologists David Schindler and John Vallentyne in their 2008 book *The Algal Bowl: The Overfertilization of the World's Freshwaters and Estuaries.*

They were particularly concerned about the rise of confined animal feeding operations (CAFOs), which can house thousands of animals in a small area. "Although there are some notable exceptions, the disposal of wastes from CAFOs is generally very primitive," they wrote. "In many cases, manure is simply piled for later application to land or washed with copious amounts of freshwater into primitive lagoons, where wastes decompose for several months before being applied to land as a liquid spray. Little attempt is made to remove pathogens, nutrients, or other contaminants from the wastes before they are re-applied to the land."

Steve Hrudey, a public health scientist, sat on the Walkerton inquiry's research advisory panel. His review of outbreaks in jurisdictions around the world showed that many of the failures that played a role in the Walkerton tragedy had also been contributing factors on other occasions. "We must take seriously the lessons learned from these experiences so as to avoid similar failures in the future," Justice O'Connor wrote about Hrudey's research.

Hrudey, associate dean of the University of Alberta's School of Public Health prior to retiring, went on to delve into the issue in more detail in a book he co-wrote in 2004 with his wife, Elizabeth. "Over the long term, the trend towards reducing serious health consequences from waterborne outbreaks has been excellent, but we seem to have fallen victim to complacency by allowing a number of serious, yet eminently preventable outbreaks to occur during the past decade," they wrote in *Safe Drinking Water: Lessons from Recent Outbreaks in Affluent Nations*. "Treatment failures, inadequate treatment and poor source selection can be used as categories to summarize most of the apparent causes," was their conclusion after discussing dozens of incidents.

The Hrudeys stress the importance of thorough, attentive treatment once the water is pulled from its source, but one of the first water safety barriers they mention is source water protection. Although completely pure water is not attainable, extremely high quality water can be found in nature, they wrote. "Far-sighted human settlements have valued such water sources because protecting this quality pays major dividends for health and quality of life of the communities they supply." Major cities like New York, Seattle and Melbourne long ago established protected drinking water supply catchments, the Hrudeys noted. These cities are now "the envy of other communities because of the consistently high quality water that they provide."

New York has been able to stave off expensive water treatment plant costs because of its clean supply. The city says it has the largest unfiltered surface water supply in the world. Every day, some 4.9 billion litres of water from this vast system is delivered to 9 million New York City and state residents, the city says. It has an active program that seeks to buy even more land in the watershed it relies on for long-term protection.

In December 2009, the city called for a prohibition on any natural gas drilling in the New York City watershed. The call was made because of a boom in the drilling of the Marcellus Shale, a gas-rich deposit that runs through several eastern states before tapering off in southern Ontario. "Natural gas drilling and exploration are incompatible with the operation of New York City's unfiltered water supply system and pose unacceptable risks for more than 9 million New Yorkers in the City and State," the city's environment department declared. Drilling in the watershed requires invasive industrialization and creates a substantial risk of chemical contamination and infrastructure damage, according to the final impact assessment report prepared for the New York City Department of Environmental Protection.

Once human developments occur in a watershed (catchment) for either surface or groundwater, the range and magnitude of water quality problems grow substantially, along with the difficulty in successfully managing them, the Hrudeys wrote. "Development, once allowed, cannot easily be reversed."

Justice O'Connor recognized the truth of that statement and recommended that a source protection plan be set up for each watershed in Ontario. He also advocated again the multi-barrier approach, the only real way of preventing human waterborne illnesses from arising. "Putting in place a series of measures, each independently acting as a barrier to passing water-borne contaminants through the system to consumers, achieves a greater overall level of protection than does relying exclusively on a single barrier (e.g., treatment alone or source protection alone). A failure in any given barrier will not cause a failure of the entire system."

O'Connor referenced the discovery made by Dr. John Snow in 1854 in London, England. After plotting cases of cholera on a map, Snow linked a water pump to an outbreak of the disease, broaching the idea that drinking water could kill people by transmitting disease. Since then, the developed world has come a long way toward eliminating the transmission of water-borne disease, O'Connor wrote. But he added, "The Walkerton experience warns us that we may have become victims of our own success, taking for granted our drinking water's safety. The keynote in the future should be vigilance. We should never be complacent about drinking water safety."

The Ontario government did follow up on his recommendations. In 2002, the government passed the Safe Drinking Water Act, which expanded on existing policy and practice and introduced new features to protect drinking water in Ontario. The government said the act would protect human health through the control and regulation of drinking water systems and drinking water testing.

The government further addressed O'Connor's concerns about source water protection with the Clean Water Act in 2006. This act requires local source protection committees to prepare science-based assessment reports for designated watershed areas. Once the committees identify and assess threats to drinking water sources, they create science-based plans outlining what actions are required to address those threats.

But this is the kind of system that only works with constant repetition. Circumstances change, O'Connor warned. "Ontario's population will likely continue increasing, as will the intensity and the types of human activities that can threaten drinking water sources. New pathogens and chemical contaminants will continue to emerge. We will be able to minimize risk to a negligible level in the future only if we constantly monitor the design and management of our water delivery systems to ensure that we are always employing the safest practices available." This statement, of course, could apply to any part of Canada that is experiencing population growth.

Shifting Safety Standards

Most—88 percent—of the water that Canadians drink comes from our lakes and rivers. Another 10 percent comes from groundwater and 2 percent is from groundwater under the direct influence of surface water, according to a Statistics Canada report. The majority of Canada's population, about 28 million people, receive their drinking water from plants that serve communities of 300 people or more. Those plants processed 5878 million cubic metres of raw water in 2007, the equivalent of over 2 million Olympic-sized swimming pools. Another 5 million Canadians have private water supplies or are serviced by smaller systems, most of which use groundwater.

Updating Guidelines

About 98 percent of plants reporting monthly E. coli results produced drinking water that never exceeded the federal guideline for drinking water. While that may sound like a great accomplishment, Health Canada actually has over 90 different chemical, microbiological and physical guidelines for drinking water. There have been 22 updates to the guidelines since 1996, adding and changing everything from E. coli to arsenic. Some of the changes have been dramatic. Arsenic, for example, had its previous limit cut by more than 50 percent. Another 16 parameters or subjects are currently undergoing reviews and public consultation, including guidance for boil-water advisories and a new guideline for benzene.

The shifting needle on what's considered safe undoubtedly adds to the uncertainty Canadians feel about their water supply. But changes have to be made when science discovers new health effects that weren't previously known. Health Canada says its priority is, generally, dealing with microbiological contaminants, such as bacteria, protozoa and viruses. Any measure taken to reduce concentrations of chemical contaminants should not compromise the effectiveness of disinfection, the department says.

Hrudey agrees with this statement. In the book he and his wife wrote, called *Safe Drinking Water: Lessons from Recent Outbreaks in Affluent Nations*, they emphasized that pathogens such as *Giardia* and *Cryptosporidium* are the greatest risk to human health via drinking water, not chemicals. The good news is that all pathogens are particles, he says. "They may get very small—viruses are really small, a lot smaller than *Cryptosporidium*, which presents different challenges in terms of removal—but it's really kind of an important thing. It doesn't really matter whether a pathogen is highly infectious or relatively noninfectious; if you get the particles out then you're getting them out."

Do all these guidelines and the changes in provincial water laws since Walkerton and North Battleford mean we're safer now? "I guess so," says Hrudey with some reluctance. "It's gotten a lot of attention. Do I think it's impossible for us to have another Walkerton? No. There are still plenty of people out there who don't get it. There are far too many people who would be prepared to dismiss Walkerton as just some incompetent guys who drank on the job." Hrudey says he's even heard regulators say that. "And they really should know better."

Recognizing the Importance of Competence

Overall there is still plenty of work to be done to ensure Canadians have a safe water supply. Hrudey says the book he and his wife wrote at one time had a subtitle that read "Lessons *Learned* from Recent Outbreaks in Affluent Nations." "But when we went to press," he explains, "we changed that to just 'lessons' because after writing up 73 case studies where it seemed like not very much was getting learned, we concluded the lessons hadn't been learned."

His main concern is that we still don't truly appreciate the importance of competence. He offers an analogy: "If you're getting on a plane you kind of like to know the guys sitting up at the front know what they're doing. And they know how to react if things go bad and that they react the right way. And collectively as an industry they've learned from their mistakes and that kind of overall emphasis on good practice and competence." Someone running a drinking water system has the capability of making the entire community sick, Hrudey points out. "So isn't this kind of an important job? And do we treat it that way? Not really."

Providing a safe water supply in a country like Canada shouldn't be difficult because we're not massively polluted and we don't have a high population density, Hrudey says. "But we still have outbreaks. So you have to ask yourself, why is that happening? It's because people aren't recognizing the way things can go wrong and not reacting the right way when things do start going wrong. It's the emphasis in people and in operating systems that's critical."

Hrudey says there needs to be more emphasis on training and the status of the people who run the system. "In a lot of places you're hiring people barely above minimum wage. They might be the same guy that sweeps the street. It's particularly a problem in smaller places." In smaller communities, the politics are such that the people who sign the cheques aren't necessarily keen on spending money that doesn't have high visibility, and unfortunately that includes training, he says.

Probably the best example of saving money gone wrong was in the North Battleford inquiry report. "It was a classic case of a small community scrimping. They took pride in the fact that they had a $700 training budget and never spent a nickel of it. The commissioner of the inquiry singled out the city administration as setting up barriers to the chance of anybody getting competent. They just took pride in the fact that they didn't allow people to get trained or learn what should be done."

Hrudey points to Australia as a leader. There, the focus is on good practice rather than just a list of water quality parameters, he says. "The reason why that's important is because the people in Walkerton, for example, if they had set about doing what they were supposed to do, the numbers were more than adequate to have the job done. The problem was they weren't doing what they were supposed to. So is that a problem of not having stringent enough numbers or is it a problem of having people not knowing what they are doing?"

Duncan Ellison of the Canadian Water and Wastewater Association says there has been a general move across the country to require mandatory certification of the operators since Walkerton. "The question is whether or not the mandatory certification to the model that is there is really appropriate. For example, in the current operator certification there is very little on some of the emerging technologies of [disinfecting with] ozone because the training is related to chlorine and chloramines, which is the traditional disinfection process."

Ellison is also worried about the oncoming wave of baby boom retirement. "That is a problem. Public servants are hitting their 60s and expect to leave…[T]he question is, are there enough younger people to take their place?" With the retirement of baby boomers will come loss of corporate memory, he adds. "Not everything is written down. They've actually had cases where water mains have broken and they couldn't find the shut off valve until they hauled a guy out of retirement. And he said, 'Yeah, 30 years ago we put a valve in there, we just didn't put it on the plan.'"

Increasing and Continuing Monitoring of Pathogens

The need for vigilance remains high, though. An article in the *Canadian Medical Association Journal* (CMAJ) in 2008 said there were, at that time, 1766 provincial boil water advisories in effect in communities and neighbourhoods across Canada. Ontario and British Columbia made up two-thirds of that number.

British Columbia's provincial health officer told the CMAJ at the time that there are more than 3500 water systems in the province, most of which deliver surface water and are untreated, so are vulnerable to potential contamination. He noted their boil water advisories had gone up over the past three or four years because of greater attention to monitoring and risk and probably an application of the turbidity guidelines.

Boil water advisories are usually issued when evidence indicates that the drinking water is or may be responsible for an outbreak of illness. The public health authority in the area may know that the water contains bacteria or parasites and that the system is unable to clean the water of those pathogens. Or it could be anticipating conditions that could result in contamination.

A website called The Water Chronicles (http://www.water.ca), run out of Ontario, also posts boil water advisories for Canada on a map. "After Walkerton, it was clear to us that a national alert system was the first step in ensuring clean drinking water and advisory transparency," says Josée Miville-Dechêne, one of the three founders of the website. "Although still a work in progress, as some official sources still display reticence in delivering information in a timely and public manner, we believe that if our [boil water advisory] maps and water alerts system can save even one life it is well worth the effort."

The Public Health Agency of Canada has a keen interest in how much of a role improperly treated water plays in causing human illness. The agency runs a pilot surveillance program called C-EnterNet that checks on the cases of infectious gastrointestinal illness and sources of exposure in the Regional Municipality of Waterloo, Ontario. This community of about 500,000 residents is a mix of urban and rural areas. It contains the Grand River, which was mentioned earlier as a spot where efforts were being made to keep manure out of the river. Yet testing of the river shows continued reason for concern. "*Cryptosporidium* and *Giardia* are consistently being detected at many of the sample locations along the river and thus continue to be an important consideration for water treatment plant operators in the watershed," says the initiative's most recent report from 2008. "The prevalence of *Giardia* contamination in the river has remained fairly stable over the past three years, while the prevalence of *Cryptosporidium* contamination shows a small decline. Nevertheless, the prevalence for both pathogens remains high in the river."

The project leaders are hoping that their approach, which studies how animals, humans and their ecosystems mesh, will help prevent and control infectious diseases. They tracked the incidence rate of 11 different intestinal diseases in the community. In 2008, citizens reported 15 cases of locally obtained cryptosporidiosis and 48 cases of giardiasis. In some cases, these diseases were caught while travelling. Those numbers may not sound high, but the cases of giardiasis went up significantly in the three-year period studied so far. And the report says that for every case of acute gastroenteritis that is counted through public health surveillance, there are an estimated 313 cases in the community that go unmeasured. The project team said in its report that four additional sites were planned to improve estimates of the burden of enteric disease in Canada.

National scale reports show intestinal parasites have more success in Yukon, British Columbia and Ontario than in other provinces and territories. The most recent report, from 2006, showed that the national rate of parasitic infections in Canada has remained relatively constant over the prior five-year period, with 16.8 cases per 100,000 people in 2006. *Giardia* was most prevalent, the report said, representing 73 percent of the parasitic infections, distantly followed by *Cryptosporidium* with 13 percent. Two other less well-known bugs made up the remaining cases.

Other Types of Water Contamination

Pharmaceuticals

A major issue that has surfaced in the water quality world is pharmaceuticals. As our ability to test our water got increasingly sophisticated, we started to find some surprising and unwelcome chemicals. This category of newly discovered intruders is generally lumped under pharmaceuticals and personal care products and includes everything from the components of our most common drugs, like birth control pills and headache remedies, to the anti-bacterial agents often found in hand soap.

Ontario's environment ministry released a study in 2010 that revealed the results of its search for pharmaceuticals in untreated and treated water. It found lots: 27 compounds were detected on at least one occasion in either untreated source water, finished drinking water or both. In untreated source water alone, 23 compounds were found. Of those, 22 compounds, including 8 pharmaceuticals, 12 antibiotics, 1 hormone and the suspected endocrine disruptor bisphenol-A, were detected in drinking water. In other words, the water treatment methods used by many drinking water plants in Ontario don't do a great job of completely removing pharmaceuticals.

Is this something we should be worried about? Both the federal and Ontario governments say that the drugs being found in our drinking water are at concentrations of parts per trillion. This concentration is far below the "therapeutic" level required to have the desired biological effect that we would take the drug for. A person would have to drink thousands of glasses of water a day to exceed an acceptable daily intake, a measure of a specific compound in drinking water that a person can drink over a life-time without an appreciable health risk, the Ontario report says.

A few other jurisdictions, including Alberta, Quebec and the Greater Vancouver Regional District, have looked for pharmaceuticals and personal care products in their water and have found them, but at this time, there are no Canadian or provincial drinking water quality guidelines for pharmaceuticals. However, some jurisdictions and research institutions have gone further to address this issue, the Ontario report says. The Netherlands and an organization called the Pharmaceutical Research and Manufacturers of America have publicly stated that there are no human health concerns associated with trace levels of pharmaceuticals in finished drinking water. Australia has set some guidelines for human and veterinary pharmaceuticals. That country, however, relies more heavily on recycled water following a drought that has stretched to 10 years in some places.

Duncan Ellison is impatiently waiting for someone in Canada to make the same declaration as the Dutch. "Nobody is willing to do what we have been asking them to do and that is to either make an upfront statement that these pharmaceuticals are not a public health concern or to really get back to the pharmacy companies and look at the amount of unused pharmaceuticals which end up being excreted from human bodies," he says. "My inclination is when you're finding the presence of these drugs in parts per billion and the prescribed dosage will be in terms of milligrams per kilogram of body weight which is in terms of thousands or tens of thousands, I'm not persuaded there is an issue." But a letter to the federal minister of health asking for a clear statement on the issue went unanswered.

Ellison does not dispute that drugs of all kinds—legal and illegal—are ending up in water supplies. "In fact there have been some really interesting articles projecting the amount of heroin and cocaine that's been consumed on the basis of the residuals found in the downstream effluents," he says. Ellison points to a study done in Italy that showed that actual cocaine use was much higher than official assumptions: wastewater surveys showed that in the Po River basin, 40,000 doses *a day* were being consumed compared to the 15,000 doses a month that was assumed to be the case.

In any case, there are all kinds of concerns about these drugs. Kristjanson, back at Lake Winnipeg, is one example of a downstream recipient who doesn't appreciate the injection of drugs into his water supply. It makes him uneasy to know that sewage is not treated to 100 percent purity. "If you take the water and if you use it, then it should be put back into the system exactly the same way as you got it," he insists. "What has to happen there is, all the pharmaceuticals have to be taken out. And I don't care what it costs! I don't care!"

Everything from Edmonton, Calgary and Saskatchewan, he says, it all ends up here. "I'm the last joker on the list." He worries how it might affect the fishery. "That has to come out. We don't want it in the flesh of the fish."

In fact, the effects of all these pharmaceuticals and personal care products appear to be much more dire for fish and frogs and other organisms immersed daily in our wastewater. It has long been known that fish exposed to synthetic estrogens, which we also know can come from wastewater treatment plants, become feminized. That is, male fish can develop early stage eggs in their testes. Although this change would obviously hamper reproduction, it wasn't clear how much of an effect it could have on a population.

But in 2007, Karen Kidd and her colleagues published a paper on research done at the Experimental Lakes Area in northern Ontario that nailed the issue. Kidd exposed the fathead minnows in one lake to synthetic estrogen at low concentrations (parts per trillion), similar to what would be found in untreated and treated municipal wastewaters. After just two seasons of estrogen additions, the fathead minnow population collapsed. During the seven-year span of the study, their population was driven to near extinction in the lake.

The estrogen appeared to have the most impact on fish with shorter life spans, but because those species, like fathead minnows, are at the bottom of the food chain, their decline can have big impacts on the whole ecosystem. Two other species—pearl dace and lake trout—that are higher up on the food chain also dropped in number. The good news was that when the estrogen supplements stopped, the minnow population recovered.

Some of the other compounds floating around in our wastewater also appear to have impacts. Scientists have found development problems in fish caused by common antidepressants such as Prozac, Zoloft and Paxil. Even antibacterial agents, which are now common in soap, might have some scary repercussions. Research out of the University of Victoria showed that low levels of the anti-microbial agent triclosan, similar to levels found in the environment, can interfere with the endocrine system of bullfrogs. The tadpoles lose weight and have trouble metamorphosizing into fully grown frogs.

A study published in 2009 showed that, higher up the food chain, 31 percent of dolphins off the coast of South Carolina and 23 percent of dolphins from Florida had triclosan in their bloodstream. This is the first study to report bioaccumulation of triclosan in a marine mammal, and it highlights the need for further monitoring and assessment, the study said.

Triclosan is showing up in people, too. The American Centers for Disease Control released its latest report on human exposure to environmental chemicals in 2009. For the first time, they tested for triclosan—and found it in almost 75 percent of their subjects. A Swedish study also found the chemical in the blood and breast milk of nursing women. Although triclosan was found in the blood and milk of all 36 women examined, concentrations were higher in the mothers who used personal care products containing triclosan than in the mothers who did not.

Aside from consuming it in everyday products, such as toothpaste, triclosan has also been found in treated drinking water in low concentrations. But scientists say endocrine disruptors don't need to be at high concentrations to have an impact. The bullfrog study, for example, found endocrine effects at 0.03 parts per billion.

It turns out that the old method of regulating chemicals, in which higher doses are assumed to cause more harm than lower doses, doesn't work when it comes to endocrine disruptors and other chemicals that mimic hormones. Scientists at the University of Missouri, Columbia, for example, found that low doses of both bisphenol-A and another endocrine disruptor called diethylstilbestrol (DES) caused significant enlargement of the adult prostate weight of mice exposed in the womb. If exposed, however, to higher doses of bisphenol-A or DES, there is no enlargement.

This field of science is called epigenetics, and it is making increasingly scary discoveries. What research is finding is that some of these compounds cause a gene to express itself differently, even though it doesn't change the underlying DNA sequence. The chemical causes changes in the molecules that are attached to DNA, and these molecules control whether a gene can be turned on. Experiments on rats have shown that some of these chemicals can pass fertility changes on to at least three subsequent generations, even though only one generation was exposed.

To top it all off, we have to keep in mind that these chemicals aren't in our water in isolation. Research has found a cocktail of chemicals in the same water samples. How they all interact is an endless puzzle, given all the different combinations and concentrations they could be found in. Research from Europe shows that sometimes one substance worsens the effect of another substance, while other times the interaction lessens the effect of a chemical.

Although wastewater treatment plants and drinking water plants do substantially reduce the concentration of pharmaceuticals and the like, they're not designed for it. Ellison doesn't think they should be required to remove these substances, anyway. "That's an end of pipe solution, whereas what we would want is a beginning of the pipe solution. We would really like pharmaceuticals to be reformulated to the extent they can be; we would like doctors to not over-prescribe. We would like people with leftover drugs not to flush them down the toilet."

When Ellison says he would like pharmaceuticals to be reformulated, he means that we should be required to have drugs that break down in the environment, rather than persist. Hrudey says pharmaceuticals are degradable. "They're not like DDT that builds up in an ecosystem." But it's not known how much damage pharmaceuticals can do to an ecosystem before they degrade. And sometimes the components that a chemical breaks down into are more harmful than the original chemical.

From a public health standpoint, though, Hrudey agrees with Ellison on the matter of harm to humans. "The simple fact is, drinking water is not a very effective vehicle for delivering health-threatening doses of very many things," he says. "It clearly can with pathogens, as we keep proving it. But the amount of pharmaceuticals you can deliver in drinking water at part-per-trillion levels is trivial." He adds, "There's a good reason why there's a concern for fish. Fish live and breathe water. That's not the same as humans that drink 2 litres a day."

So why don't the health authorities reassure us by telling us we have nothing to worry about? Hrudey says they're afraid to. "Health authorities work for governments, and governments are run by politicians. And politicians at every level are very skittish about having their civil servants making pronouncements that might be held against them at some point. Particularly at the federal level."

Environment Canada has been studying the matter. One of the interesting facts noted at a 2007 workshop on the topic was that pharmaceuticals are more water soluble, while personal care products are designed for external use and tend to be more fat soluble. What this means is that the fat soluble chemicals will be able to accumulate in animals. It was suggested at the workshop that this made it easier to justify restrictions on the use of problematic ingredients in personal care products than on the use of pharmaceuticals. However, environmental groups note that if a water soluble pharmaceutical is constantly replenished by sewage outlets, it, too, would qualify as being persistent in the environment.

Certain kinds of treatment are more effective at removing pharmaceuticals, such as ozonation, activated carbon and nanofiltration, the experts at the workshop said. They also concluded that the consumption of drinking water, even if it contained the highest concentration of individual pharmaceuticals reported for drinking water, is very unlikely to cause negative effects—based on the current knowledge.

Pesticides and Herbicides

An estimated 20 million kilograms of pesticides and herbicides are applied to crops on the Canadian Prairies every year, according to Environment Canada. It would not be shocking to find them in the surrounding waterways. And indeed, generally where there is conventional agriculture, there are pesticides and herbicides in the water. Groundwater in agricultural areas can also be contaminated. In Alberta, the Oldman, Red Deer and Battle rivers had pesticide concentrations that exceeded guidelines in the 2007–2008 testing period.

In some areas, the use of pesticides and herbicides is growing. The chemicals were applied to over 10,516 square kilometres of Quebec in 2006, or 49 percent more than in 1996, according to Statistics Canada. Environment Canada scientists have been studying pesticides in the St. Lawrence River near Quebec City and at the mouths of some tributaries of Lake Saint-Pierre. The St. Lawrence River, especially Lake Saint-Pierre, is vulnerable to contamination by pesticides and herbicides because several tributaries draining farming areas empty into it, they say. The Yamaska River basin has the highest proportion of farmland, and this is where they found the highest number of pesticides—at the mouth of the Yamaska River. The biggest source of pesticide contamination in the St. Lawrence River turned out to be the Great Lakes. Environment Canada's test results found that Lake Ontario was the source of 90 percent of a type of pesticide called triazines measured in the St. Lawrence River in the 1990s.

Most pesticide concentrations in the aquatic environment were within quality criteria. However, quality criteria for the protection of aquatic life in the Nicolet and Saint-François rivers are sometimes exceeded by concentrations of chlorpyrifos, an organophosphorous insecticide widely used for mosquito control, they found. Chlorpyrifos tends to bioaccumulate in fish and algae.

Another issue with pesticides and herbicides in water supplies is that it can be a problem for irrigators. In the study area, irrigation is required primarily for vegetable production and ornamental production. "When pesticide concentrations exceed the criteria for agricultural irrigation, it becomes risky to use the water as an irrigation source since it could damage crops," the report says.

Some of these chemicals, it turns out, can also cause fertility defects in animals. One study that looked at a fungicide and a pesticide found that the two chemicals caused fertility defects in male rats that are passed down to nearly every male in subsequent generations. A 2010 study published in the prestigious *Proceedings of the National Academy of Sciences* showed that the commonly applied herbicide atrazine both demasculinized (chemically castrated) and completely feminized exposed male frogs.

Trichloroethylene

As if pharmaceuticals and pesticides and herbicides are not enough, there are plenty of other types of contamination around. The residents of Shannon, Quebec, have been worried about an industrial degreasing agent called trichloroethylene (TCE), which has been found in some groundwater wells adjacent to Canadian Forces Garrison Valcartier. Health Canada says the chemical is possibly carcinogenic to humans. Rats exposed to TCE have developed kidney and testicular tumours, while exposed mice get pulmonary and liver tumours, the agency says. "Studies in humans seem to support these links, but further studies are needed to confirm them, in part because other chemicals were also present."

The fight in Shannon has been going on for at least the past 13 years. The Department of National Defence (DND) began studying the problem in 1997 when it discovered TCE in the aquifer below the garrison. "As a result of these investigations, sources of TCE in the groundwater have been discovered at Defence R&D Canada—Valcartier, and on an adjacent property belonging to SNC Technologies Inc.," says a department press release dated February 2010.

The Municipality of Shannon sued the federal government and SNC in 2003. Within a matter of months, the issue was settled out of court. "Without admitting liability, DND agreed to provide $19 million to the Municipality of Shannon for the development of a potable water supply and connection of homes to this supply," the department said. In 2009, the federal government spent another $13.3 million to complete construction of new water mains in Shannon, though they said this move was unrelated to the lawsuit.

A class action lawsuit by residents is currently underway. The Quebec Superior Court authorized Marie-Paule Spieser to begin the class action on behalf of anyone who has lived in the municipality after 1953 and was affected by the TCE in the groundwater.

About 3000 people joined the suit, with damages estimated at $2 billion. That amount covers everything from damage to physical and mental health, to loss of wells and increased municipal taxes.

The federal government filed its statement of defence in early 2010, saying, among other things, that it did not commit any fault and even if it did, there is no causal link between the alleged contamination and the alleged health problems. It added that the plaintiffs' data indicates only 40 wells showed a TCE concentration greater than Health Canada's recommended level of concentration in drinking water.

Tritium

Canada's nuclear industry throws another water contaminant into the mix in the form of tritium, a radioactive form of hydrogen. Tritium does form naturally in the upper atmosphere when cosmic rays collide with gas in the atmosphere. It makes its way down to earth in rain, but it remains at low concentrations.

> The half-life of tritium is 12.33 years: it takes just over 12 years for the radioactivity to be reduced by half, another 12 years to be reduced by one-quarter, and so on, until it has all eventually changed to helium, a stable, non-radioactive element.

In Canada, non-atmospheric tritium is generated from fission of uranium in reactor fuel, says the Canadian Nuclear Safety Commission, the country's nuclear regulator. It's also created from neutron irradiation of heavy water. Heavy water, unlike regular water, is created from oxygen and another naturally occurring hydrogen isotope called deuterium. Heavy water is used in some nuclear reactors such as the Canadian CANDU reactor, the commission says. Most tritium emitted by Canadian nuclear reactors is in the form of tritiated water.

In atmospheric moisture, the concentration of natural tritium is about 0.2 to 1.0 becquerels per litre (a becquerel is a unit of radioactivity that measures one unit of disintegration per second). In public drinking water supplies found close to nuclear facilities, concentrations are typically in the range of less than 1.9 to 209 becquerels per litre, the commission says. When someone drinks this tritiated water, half of the tritium is excreted in 10 days. However, a small amount does become bound to proteins, fat and carbohydrates in the body with an average 40-day half life, the commission says.

While the commission insists the general population in Canada is not at risk from tritium intake, environmental groups and others with specific worries about tritium have mobilized and become increasingly vocal about the isotope. "Tritium replaces ordinary non-radioactive hydrogen and travels throughout the body, going wherever water goes," warned the Sierra Club of Canada in a 2009 report. "It becomes part of our DNA—and that's where it does its damage, from close range. Tritium decays within our body, ejecting high velocity beta particles that can break the chemical bonds of our DNA. The result can be cancer or birth defects. A developing fetus is particularly susceptible to damage from exposure to radiation."

The commission fired back right away, calling the Sierra Club's report "junk science" and accusing them of needlessly scaring the public. "For instance, the Sierra Club concludes that current tritium levels cause birth defects and increase cancer risk, which is *not* the case," the commission said in its press release.

The Sierra Club said there have been frequent leaks of radioactive water from the National Research Universal (NRU) reactor at Chalk River, Ontario. Atomic Energy of Canada Limited (AECL) collects the radioactive water and dumps it into the Ottawa River. From December 2008 to February 2009, AECL deliberately released 30 trillion becquerels of tritium into the river.

But the commission says drinking water supplies are safe and tritium levels are well below Health Canada's drinking water quality guideline for tritium, which is 7000 becquerels per litre. The City of Ottawa, which is downstream of Chalk River, also felt a need to respond, and reassured its residents that their drinking water is safe to drink and well below the standards established by Health Canada. It then published its tritium test results for the last three years online. Averages were single digits readings, but the ranges did hit as high as 30 becquerels per litre.

While those results show a lot of breathing room under the current Health Canada guideline of 7000 becquerels per litre, Ontario is in the process of re-examining that limit. The review was triggered in 2007 by Ontario's environment minister, who received a request from the City of Toronto's medical officer of health. The Ontario Drinking Water Advisory Council was handed the job. The council was asked to review a 1994 report from the former Ontario Advisory Committee on Environmental Standards, which recommended a standard of 100 becquerels per litre, to be further reduced to 20 becquerels per litre after five years. That recommendation was not adopted at the time.

Later in 2007, Greenpeace released a report on tritium, and the council was asked by the environment minister to take that report into account, as well. The author of that report was Ian Fairlie, an independent consultant on radioactivity in the environment who has degrees in chemistry and in radiation biology. He wrote that tritium levels in those Great Lakes with nuclear reactors on their shores are two to five times greater than in Lake Superior, which has no reactors. He added that the tritium level in Lake Ontario is increasing each year, mainly due to CANDU discharges and to major tritium leaks in past years. "Tritium concentrations in drinking water, in air, and in vegetation and food near CANDU stations are all significantly increased," Fairlie warned. "These result in turn in high tritium intakes in residents living within 5 to 10 kilometres of CANDU stations and very high tritium annual intakes in residents who live within 1 to 2 kilometres of the CANDU stations."

He suggested the federal and Ontario governments should re-examine the risks associated with tritium, as well as how tritium doses are measured. Among the more alarming recommendations, perhaps, was that pregnant women and children under four years old should be advised not to live within 10 kilometres of tritium-emitting facilities and that people who live within 5 kilometres of such facilities should be advised not to consume food from their own gardens, bee hives and orchards, and not to consume wild foods, e.g., blackberries and mushrooms, growing very near the facilities.

In the end, the council recommended the Ontario Drinking Water Quality Standard for tritium should be revised to 20 becquerels per litre. This would be calculated as the running average of the preceding 52 weekly composite samples.

No final decision had been made by the Ontario government at the time of writing.

Taking the Measure of Safety

With all these challenges to drinking water quality, Canadians can be excused for occasionally hesitating before pouring themselves a tall glass from the tap. Apparently, that hesitation spread when word got out that Health Canada was conducting a survey of tap water and water treatment facilities across the country. The agency posted a statement on its website, reassuring citizens that drinking water in Canada is amongst the safest in the world. Health Canada called the survey part of its "routine monitoring processes" but then added that similar but smaller surveys were conducted in 1976–1977 and 1993.

The survey began in January 2009 and is supposed to wrap up in 2010, with results being released to the public the following year. More than 100 different water quality parameters will be analyzed in approximately 60 water treatment facilities across the country, Health Canada says. The department does not name the facilities that were chosen, instead saying that utilities participating in the study were chosen based on criteria such as size of population served, type of treatment technology/processes, and type of source water (ground vs. surface).

At each of the sites, a number of raw and treated water samples will be collected for various tests. For some parameters, up to three additional samples will be taken from various areas within the distribution system. Each site will be sampled twice, once under winter conditions and again during summer. The samples will be preserved and shipped to the laboratories for analysis. The parameters they're looking at include a variety of disinfection by-products (54 in total); some new and emerging contaminants such as pharmaceuticals, personal care products and bisphenol-A; various inorganic substances; and general water quality. The results will help the department set priorities for drinking water guideline development. And the department will find out if it needs to put in place more measures to reduce any risks.

The disinfection by-products that Health Canada is looking at form when disinfectants such as chlorine react with bits of naturally occurring organic matter such as decaying leaves and vegetation. At least one of the by-products, chloroform, is considered to be a possible carcinogen in humans. The department believes, though, that health risks from disinfection by-products are much less than the risks from consuming water that has not been disinfected. They took a stronger stance on bisphenol-A, though, adding it to the roster of toxic substances in 2010.

CHAPTER THREE

Solution in a Bottle?

IN THE MEANTIME, THERE are many Canadians who have added what they consider an extra safety precaution to their drinking water. As we watch the battles to clean up the country's rivers and lakes and continue to hear about occasional water-related illness outbreaks, our perception of our drinking water becomes tainted. What filters down, perhaps, is that all is not as clean as it could be. The Canadian Water Attitudes survey in 2010 reflects this perception. It showed that only 49 percent of Canadians drink water directly from the tap in their home.

Steve Hrudey isn't surprised by this figure. But he says it isn't the quality of the water utility that's responsible for that trend. "It's the misunderstanding that's sort of out there and it's driven by…the bottled water people and their very well done ads. They convince people they're going to be poisoned by their water if they don't pay to get it out of a bottle. There's virtually no evidence to support any of those scare stories or impressions." Other than cases like Walkerton and North Battleford, he adds. "It really isn't a risk in Edmonton or Toronto or Ottawa or places like that." He allows that there could be a greater risk in small communities and that maybe those are the people who should be buying bottled water.

Controversial as it may be, there's no denying bottled water has found a niche on our pantry shelves. From 1998 to 2006, annual per capita consumption of bottled water increased from 28.4 litres to 66 litres, with a notable increase of 12.2 percent from 2005 to 2006, according to an Agriculture and Agri-Food Canada report. By 2007, 30 percent of households drank predominantly bottled water, whether they had a municipal or private water supply, Statistics Canada says. The rest consumed water from the tap or from both the tap and bottles.

Questionable Superiority

Bottled water has an excellent safety record in Canada, Health Canada claims. "At the present time, no waterborne disease outbreaks have been associated with drinking bottled water in Canada." The department says it is confident that the current bottled water regulations are adequate to ensure the safety of bottled water products in Canada. And yet, since 2002, Health Canada has conducted public opinion research and focus groups, workshops, targeted consultations and yet more discussion groups on these regulations. The goal is to update current requirements to incorporate new scientific knowledge, to harmonize them with the standards of other governments and international agencies and to bring the regulations in line with the Guidelines for Canadian Drinking Water Quality.

A comments document from 2008 shows there's quite a bit of jockeying for changes in labelling to differentiate mineral and spring water from other types sourced from more mundane origins, like municipal water systems. The Canadian Bottled Water Association emphasizes that products that use municipal water supplies as source water further process the water using reverse osmosis, micro-filtration, distillation, disinfection or any other appropriate measures to remove any chemical and microbiological contaminants that may be present. The finished bottled water product is completely different than the original municipal water supply after processing, the association says.

One proposed regulatory change that got a lot of backlash was lowering the maximum allowable concentration for arsenic in bottled water from 10 parts per billion to 5 parts per billion. The outcome of all this consultation is not clear yet.

The Polaris Institute, a national think tank and activist organization, says bottled water has numerous flaws. Among them, independent scientific studies have found toxic contaminants in bottled water products, including antimony leaching from PET plastic. The Canadian Food Inspection Agency has issued 29 separate recalls of 49 bottled water products since 2000, the institute said in a 2009 report.

Then C-Crest Laboratories, an accredited laboratory that specializes in pharmaceutical product testing and regulatory affairs, weighed in with a shocking study in May 2010. They initiated their own study after one of their employees consumed a bottle of water and got sick. "Several brands of bottled water, irrespective of their sources and packaging formats, were randomly purchased from the marketplace and subjected to microbiological analyses," the company said. "Surprisingly, it was discovered that more than 40 percent of the famous brands tested did not meet the [United States Pharmacopeia] specifications for drinking water. Heterotrophic bacteria counts in some of the bottles were found to be in revolting figures of one hundred times more than the permitted limit. Although the presence of Coliforms (indicator of fecal contamination) and other known pathogens was not confirmed, bacterial colonies of different morphologies were isolated from water." The Canadian Bottled Water Association expressed neither surprise nor alarm at the findings. They told media that heterotrophic bacteria are not significant from a health risk standpoint and that fresh fruit and vegetables would show the same results.

The Business of Bottled Water

Canadian bottled water companies have done quite well in the recent past, though, especially in exports. From 1996 to 2002, Canada's exports of bottled water increased sharply from a value of $130.5 million to $284.3 million, Agriculture and Agri-Food Canada says. Canada's image as an environment with pure water resources and a lower valued Canadian dollar gave these products a competitive edge. The value of exports declined significantly to $57.4 million in 2007, though, due to the rising value of the Canadian dollar, which makes domestic product more expensive relative to its competitors in other countries.

Meanwhile, Canada's imports of bottled water followed an opposite trend, increasing from $25.6 million in 1996 to $75 million in 2007. Canadian Bottled Water Association executive director Elizabeth Griswold, in a 2009 issue of *Canadian Restaurant and Foodservice News*, says the increase of bottled water consumption isn't due to consumers opting for it as a replacement to tap water. "Rather, they are turning to it as a substitute for other packaged beverages as part of a healthier lifestyle," she wrote.

In 2006, bottled water did surpass fruit/vegetable juice to become the second largest beverage sector by volume, Agriculture Canada confirms. "By 2011, bottled water is expected to challenge the volume of soft drinks sold in Canada," the department says in its report. It added, "The industry expects double digit annual growth for the next five years as consumers become more concerned about the quality of municipal water." According to Euromonitor International, bottled water sales in Canada are expected to reach a record volume of cumulative average growth rate of 13 percent over the forecast period of 2006 to 2011.

The Polaris Institute finds the trend alarming. "Public access to affordable, reliable, and safe drinking water distinguishes industrialized countries, such as Canada, the United States, Australia, and those of the European Union, from much of the rest of the world," says a Polaris report. "Despite this, the bottled water industry has grown to a multi-million dollar industry in Canada, outpacing the consumption of tea, coffee, apple juice and milk. Yet bottled water is estimated to be between 240 and 10,000 times more expensive than tap water."

But bottled water faces a number of challenges. For one thing, it's been hammered on the environment front for many years now. Bottled water production wastes energy, as does the transporting of the heavy, finished product, critics say. All of that contributes to greenhouse gas emissions. And the plastic bottles, because they're so portable and used in so many places, usually don't get recycled. Empty water bottles are commonly found in roadside ditches, parks and waterways.

Some of the more enviro-oriented, and often swank, restaurants in the U.S. and Canada began pitching their fancy bottled waters and serving what was always on tap. Universities and municipalities began rumbling about expelling bottled water from their domains.

In 2009, the Federation of Canadian Municipalities passed a resolution proposed by the cities of Toronto and London to encourage members to phase out the sale and purchase of bottled water at their own facilities, where potable water is available. Aside from the unnecessary fossil fuel consumption associated with bottled water, the federation said 40 to 80 percent of empty bottles end up in landfills.

The Polaris Institute, which has been monitoring the situation, said in December 2009 that 72 municipalities from eight provinces and two territories have implemented restrictions on bottled water. Of the 72 municipalities, 11 passed complete bans on bottled water (meaning that in all city facilities with potable drinking water, bottled water will no longer be sold or provided), 38 implemented widespread restrictions to cover the sale and provision in most city facilities, and 23 implemented specific restrictions (such as a ban on the sale and provision in City Halls), wrote Joe Cressy of the institute.

The Cost of Aesthetic Improvement

Although many people might agree that relying on bottled water to quench all drinking water needs is not a great idea, the numbers bear out that many people want that extra bit of treatment. Among those with a municipal water supply, the proportion of households that treat their drinking water has continued to rise, from 48 percent in 2006 to 54 percent in 2007, according to a Statistics Canada report. In 2007, 43 percent of households on a municipal water supply that treated their drinking water said they did so to address concerns about possible bacterial contamination. The majority of those with a municipal water supply treated their water to improve the taste or appearance.

Steve Hrudey believes municipal drinking water providers have to keep this craving for crystal clear, completely tasteless and odourless water in mind. He thinks a big factor driving the high percentage of people to bottled water and water treatment devices is the aesthetic quality of water. People are willing to pay 1000 times more for their bottled water simply because they don't like a chlorine smell, he says. "I don't really have a problem with that as long as people understand they're doing it for that reason. If they think they're buying improved health then they're being misled. But given that it is such a powerful driver, aesthetic characteristics is something every consumer can respond to. So the water business has to take that seriously. If they don't get on top of the aesthetic quality of their water, if they just sort of say 'It doesn't matter, we know it's safe'—that's not good enough."

Hrudey wants consumers to know that they shouldn't be consuming bottled water for safety reasons. But that's exactly what some organizations fear. "The bottled water industry's marketing of 'safe, clean water' undermines citizen's confidence in public water systems, and paves the way for the water companies to take over under-funded public utilities," says the Polaris Institute in a report that outlines numerous concerns about bottled water. "In return, public willingness to pay premium prices for bottled water enables water service corporations to establish top dollar price."

These high costs come into focus more clearly when compared to the cost of tap water, which is more difficult for people to translate because the utility bill they get doesn't break the cost down. The institute did, though: in most Canadian cities, one could re-fill their glass over 50 times with tap water for less than $0.01.

The Polaris Institute's campaign against bottled water has broad support, attracting the likes of Kairos, an interfaith activism group, and the Council of Canadians. "The world's largest for-profit water service corporations have set their sights on North America: Suez and Veolia from France and RWE–Thames from Germany are eager to deliver privatized water services, and companies like these are targeting the home/office bottled water market," the institute warns.

PART TWO

Water Governance

FOR ME, GROWING UP ON the Prairies, a water fight meant balloons filled to bursting, squirt guns and lots of giggling. Invariably, whoever took control of the garden hose—with its long range and endless supply—was the victor. In the adult world, life isn't much different. What can we do without water? Agriculture, industry, ecosystems—water plays a key role in everything. And so, no matter how creative we get in how it's used, whoever has control over the greatest quantity tends to thrive.

Unlike in those carefree childhood days, there's a lot less laughing about water management in adulthood, with lives hanging in the balance in many parts of the world. The United Nations Development Programme says the management of water resources is central to poverty alleviation and human and ecosystem health. "Currently, over one billion people lack access to water and over 2.4 billion lack access to basic sanitation," the agency says. "This water crisis is largely our own making. It has resulted not from the natural limitations of the water supply or lack of financing and appropriate technologies, even though these are important factors, but rather from profound failures in water governance."

It's a damning indictment, one that Canadians, with our growing population, thirsty neighbours and changing climate, should heed.

Water governance is a multi-pronged term that covers all the social, economic, political and administrative tactics we use to manage this precious resource. In Canada, water governance is deeply complicated, of course. As a federation, our Russian doll-within-a-doll approach to all things jurisdictional means that at least three levels of government get involved in some aspect of water management. These days, community-level watershed groups are also often asked to wade into management matters.

CHAPTER FOUR

Federal Water Governance

THE BIGGEST UMBRELLA is, of course, the federal government. At that level, over 20 departments and agencies dip their oars into water matters. Federal jurisdiction encompasses fisheries, navigation, federal lands and international relations, including responsibilities that go with managing the boundary waters shared with the United States. On top of that, there are responsibilities in the areas of agriculture, health and the environment. The federal government also manages water resources in the Northwest Territories and Nunavut as part of the mandate of Indian and Northern Affairs Canada. Yukon took over the responsibility for its own water in 2003.

Key Federal Legislation

There is a strong argument to be made in favour of federal involvement in managing our water because rivers, lakes and streams often do not fall neatly within the boundaries of one province—or even one country, as is the case near the Canada–U.S. border. Some of the critical legislation that the federal government uses to manage water matters includes the Canada Water Act and the Fisheries Act, among others.

The Canada Water Act

The Canada Water Act of 1970 acknowledges that demands on water resources and pollution of those resources are increasing rapidly and that it "has become a matter of urgent national concern that measures be taken to provide for water quality management in those areas of Canada most critically affected." This piece of legislation is supposed to allow the federal government to manage the country's water resources, including research, conservation, development and usage—all preferably with the cooperation of the provincial governments.

"It's always been a negotiation between the two levels of government, the two senior governments, in terms of who's doing what," says Rob de Loë, research chair in water policy and governance at the University of Waterloo. "Over the last century there's been a fair bit of movement on this. There was a time, after the Second World War, where the federal government was in the business of building, owning and operating large water projects. Those days are long gone. There was a time early in Canada's history when the provinces were weak and disorganized and the state, when it came to water responsibilities, was the federal government."

The Prairie Provinces actually didn't get control of their natural resources, including water, until 1930.

The Fisheries Act

The federal government maintained control, though, over fishing zones, territorial seas and inland waters of Canada through the Fisheries Act, which dates back to Confederation. This act is, theoretically at least, a potent one, as it supersedes provincial legislation when the two conflict. Its most formidable section states, "No person shall carry on any work or undertaking that results in the harmful alteration, disruption or destruction of fish habitat."

"The Fisheries Act has sometimes been characterized as the most powerful piece of environmental legislation in Canada," de Loë says. "Can you imagine an activity that doesn't affect fish or fish habitat? Good luck." The catch is, you can have all the legislation in the world, but if you fail to put in place all the things that turn legislation from paper into reality, it doesn't really matter, he says. So, for example, if you lack the political will to enforce legislation and you underfund key sections such as licensing, inspection and enforcement, the laws become useless.

The Department of Fisheries and Oceans (DFO) says that while the federal government has the authority to manage fish habitat, it has essentially no control over the use of inland waters, beds of watercourses or shorelines, which fall under provincial jurisdiction. Alternatively, the provinces cannot make regulatory decisions concerning fish habitat.

In 1999, the federal government began to increase the DFO's presence, notably in the Prairies, Ontario and Quebec, to "strengthen the department's capacity to administer and enforce the habitat protection provisions of the Fisheries Act in the inland provinces," it said. This move was largely tied to a court case that revolved around the Oldman River Dam in southern Alberta. Environmentalists went to the Supreme Court of Canada, which ruled that the federal government must perform environmental assessments for all projects needing federal permits. The courts also determined that habitat protection under the Fisheries Act cannot be delegated to the provinces. In response, the department increased the number of offices in its Prairies region, adding seven around 2002. It's thought that much of this expansion has been clawed back since then, but despite being given five months, DFO could not or would not say how the number of offices and the number of staff have changed in the last 10 years.

The Canadian Environmental Protection Act

Another keystone piece of legislation is the Canadian Environmental Protection Act. Its big role is pollution prevention. Enforcing this act requires a great love of lists. To keep track of what should not be getting into the environment, the act has a registry of substances. This registry is broken down into inventories, or lists. There's a list of domestic substances, a list of export control substances, a list of priority substances, a list of toxic substances, and so on.

The list of domestic substances is the longest, stretching to about 23,000 entries. Most are chemicals that were being used in Canada between 1984 and 1986. The list has been amended regularly since then to include additional substances. Procedures have changed since the list was first cobbled together, though. Since 1994, Canada has been screening all new chemical substances before allowing their use.

Many of the chemical substances introduced before 1994 had not been examined by environmental and health scientists in government for their potential risks. The government is trying to remedy that. They began by categorizing the domestic substance list. That is, they broke the list down into more lists. The categorization work looked for chemicals that were inherently toxic to humans or to the environment and that might be persistent (i.e., take a very long time to break down) and/or bioaccumulative. They also looked for substances to which people might have the greatest potential for exposure.

It turns out that approximately 4300 of Canada's 23,000 existing substances needed further attention, including screening assessments, research and, if needed, measures to control the use of a chemical substance. Among the 4300, another list of 200 turned out to be of the highest priority. These high-priority ones in turn were divided into 12 smaller batches. The chemicals in these batches that are identified as persistent, bioaccumulative and inherently toxic to aquatic organisms will be up for possible elimination. Final decisions on all 12 batches were scheduled to be made by the end of 2011.

The Navigable Waters Protection Act

Another piece of federal legislation that applies to the fresh-water realm is the Navigable Waters Protection Act, which dates back to 1882. This act controls what is built or placed in, on, over, under, through or across any navigable water. Nothing can be put there without prior permission from the federal government.

The Federal Water Policy

In 1987, the Federal Water Policy was released. The environment minister at the time, Tom McMillan, shared some emphatic sentiments in the introduction. First, he reviewed the country's paradox, that though the country has lots of water, most of it is not in the populated areas of the country. That situation is compounded by drought in certain regions. "Put simply, Canada is not a water-rich country," he wrote.

He continued: "We must manage water like any other valuable resource—with care. The object should be to use it in our own time in a way that leaves it unimpaired for our children and their children after them. Most of all, we must recognize its worth."

The policy said the federal government would encourage pricing and other strategies, such as the beneficiary/polluter pays concept, to encourage efficient water use. McMillan wrote that the Federal Water Policy "calls for a radically new attitude toward Canada's water—one that attaches real value to the resource itself. The policy also recognizes the need for a more open style of decision making in this area. Because the public gains when policies work and suffers when they don't, it makes sense for the government to involve Canadians in every facet of water management."

The policy's two main goals are to protect and enhance the quality of the water resource and to promote the wise and efficient management and use of water. But it also stresses that government action is not enough. "Canadians at large must become aware of the true value of water in their daily lives and use it wisely."

Unfortunately, the Federal Water Policy is effectively defunct, says de Loë. "It was a great policy," he says. "For its time, it was thoughtful and well developed and there was lots of consultation. A lot of the ideas still make a lot of sense—but the policy was not implemented. So from my point of view, what is the federal government's water policy? It seems to be that the policy is to not have a comprehensive policy. The fact that the 1987 Federal Water Policy still can be downloaded from the government's website is really quite beside the point."

Strangely enough, the federal government kept the policy on their website when they rewrote everything "stem to stern" on their water pages in early 2010. "I guess if they took it down completely it would be signalling defeat," de Loë says.

Federal Holdings

Another area of water jurisdiction for the federal government that happens to be one of the more straightforward ones is managing water on federal lands and in federal buildings. The federal government says it is the largest landowner in Canada. It owns or leases more than 25,000 properties across Canada with a total land area of over 30 million hectares. This includes national parks, wildlife areas, federal office buildings, labs, penitentiaries and military bases. In addition, there are 240 million hectares of federal crown land in Nunavut and the Northwest Territories. Although the exact amount no doubt changes over time, the government also recently claimed to own over 30 million square metres of floor area in more than 46,000 buildings across the country. Water in all these holdings must be used efficiently and wastewater managed appropriately.

The "Watered Down" Report

In spite of all its various powers and pieces of legislation, the federal government comes under frequent attack in all corners of the country for failing to protect water resources. In October 2009, seven environmental groups criticized the government for failing to enforce and implement numerous laws that are in place to protect the water—in many cases the drinking water—for tens of thousands of Canadians who live near oilsands operations. Their report, called *Watered Down: Overcoming Federal Inaction on the Impact of Oil Sands Development to Water Resources*, identified 10 areas where the federal government has failed either to enforce or implement federal law or to exercise its constitutional authority. These areas include failure to enforce water diversions, failure to regulate toxic pollution, failure to prosecute leaking tailings ponds and failure to implement legislation to reduce acid rain from oilsands operations.

Among the recommendations in the report was a call for an immediate, comprehensive peer-reviewed assessment of the health impacts of industrial development, including all oilsands projects, on downstream residents. Among those worried about the effects are people living in Fort Chipewyan, the Mikisew Cree, the Athabasca Chipewyan and the Métis Local 125. The study, the groups said, should determine the immediate and long-term effects of contaminants in water sources, including water for domestic purposes such as bathing, cooking and drinking.

First Nations Water Management

As discussed earlier in this book, the management of drinking water and wastewater on First Nations reserves is a responsibility of the federal government. That responsibility is shared between the First Nations band councils, Indian and Northern Affairs Canada and Health Canada. Environment Canada plays an advisory role.

The Constitution Act of 1982 has a specific clause in it that recognizes and affirms existing aboriginal rights and treaty rights. Those rights include certain customs and practices. The clause means that any rights, including water rights, not extinguished before 1982 can no longer be infringed upon by the government, according to the Program on Water Governance at the University of British Columbia. This may turn into future court challenges in areas where aboriginal peoples have concerns about water quantity or quality, such as in southern Alberta or in the Northwest Territories.

For now, inadequate drinking water is a dominant concern. In its 2010 budget, the federal Conservative Party patted itself on the back, saying it had made significant progress over the last two years in improving water conditions on reserves across Canada. To build on this progress, it was going to extend the First Nations Water and Wastewater Action Plan for two more years.

Significant Risks Remain

For some critics, the improvements are not coming fast enough, and progress is expected to come only after some major regulatory changes are made. Edmonton NDP MP Linda Duncan, who also happens to be an environmental lawyer, and her friend Marie-Ann Bowden, a law professor at the University of Saskatchewan, published a book in 2009 on the predicament of First Nations when it comes to their right to clean drinking water. The book, called

A Legal Guide to Aboriginal Drinking Water: A Prairie Perspective, explains that First Nations communities do not have the same legal protections for safe drinking water as non–First Nations communities.

"Right now there are only federal guidelines under Health Canada," Duncan told me when I wrote an article about it for the *Edmonton Journal*. "Those become binding in law when the provinces incorporate those standards into their statutes and permits. So because the provincial law does not apply to reserves, they have no legal protection."

In 2001, Indian and Northern Affairs Canada found a significant risk to the quality or safety of drinking water in three-quarters of the drinking water systems in First Nations communities, says the most recent report on the issue written by the Commissioner of the Environment and Sustainable Development in 2005. In spite of the hundreds of millions of dollars spent on the issue in recent years, there are still many communities that can't produce their own potable water. The report recommends that a regulatory regime be developed for drinking water in these communities.

Duncan waited impatiently for this legislation, and the federal government finally introduced it in May 2010. The Safe Drinking Water for First Nations Act would allow the federal government to develop federal regulations for drinking water and wastewater. These regulations would apply in First Nations communities. Because provinces and territories have existing regulations governing drinking water and wastewater, the federal government said it would review these regulations to see which of them could be adapted into federal regulations. They also said they would recognize the unique water challenges facing many First Nations communities.

Before the legislation was introduced, Duncan had discovered that Indian Affairs told First Nations communities that the government would give them some money to treat their drinking water, but they would have to sign an agreement saying the communities assume all liability. "This is an issue the First Nations communities have been raising all along. They don't have the capacity, they don't have the capability, they don't have the resources. So while they welcome a new law, they're not in favour of it if it's simply going to transfer over all liability to them without the appropriate training and resources."

The federal government said it recognizes that many First Nations communities face unique water challenges and that the ability to meet federal regulatory requirements may vary from place to place. So they are going to seek a phased-in approach for regulations so that implementation coincides with a community's ability to meet regulatory requirements.

Before the bill was released, Bowden said having federal regulations is going to be an expensive proposition. "Once you decide that you have to have safe drinking water on reserves, then you have to follow through and make sure it happens. And that's the expense I'm talking about." She also said that it's also a multi-jurisdictional issue and has been something of a political hot potato.

Duncan said the issue should be looked at from source to tap, pointing out that when it's not, communities such as Fort Chipewyan in northern Alberta and the Paul Band at Wabamun Lake, west of Edmonton, end up with serious water quality concerns. "One of the biggest expenses for First Nations communities in trying to treat water is because of the contamination of their source water. A lot of First Nations communities draw their water from rivers, from lakes, also from groundwater, where there's oil and gas activity where it can potentially be contaminated. So I also talk in the book about the obligation of the government to also step up to the plate and start exerting federal authority to actually protect those source waters."

Boiling Point: a Report on Progress (or the Lack Thereof)

The First Nations Water Management Strategy that was announced in 2003 claims to take a "source to tap" approach to water management by monitoring and protecting this vital resource every step of the way—from the source, through treatment and distribution, to use and wastewater management. But frustration continues to simmer in First Nations communities.

In 2008, the Polaris Institute along with the Assembly of First Nations (AFN) and the Canadian Labour Congress issued a report on the water crisis facing First Nations called *Boiling Point! Six community profiles of the water crisis facing First Nations within Canada*. In the foreword, AFN national chief Phil Fontaine said, "First Nations continue to be frustrated by the lack of real progress being made in addressing the shameful conditions of many First Nations communities. The government's recent Action Plan Report obscures the fact that very little progress has been made on the fundamental issues facing First Nations access to safe drinking water. The United Nations Committee on Economic, Social and Cultural Rights adopted the human right to water in 2002. And yet, in 2008, at least 85 First Nations water systems are in high risk and there are close to 100 boil-water advisories in various communities."

The report highlighted six communities where the quest for clean water remained unfinished, saying, "In one profile, the community's water is tainted with uranium; another had unacceptable levels of disease-causing bacteria. Residents complain of brown water coming out of taps with a foul smell and water that stains metal. The downstream from the tar sands location of a First Nations' community causes serious concerns over the safety of source water, including disturbingly high rates of cancer and evidence of fish deformities. In another case, 90 percent of a community continues to be unconnected to a water treatment facility built by the Indian and Northern Affairs Canada in 1995."

In the report, a member of the Yellow Quill First Nation described her community's long struggle for clean drinking water as partly a result of "jurisdictional squabbling." The report reiterates that the federal government has a fiduciary responsibility to the continued health and safety of First Nations as guaranteed by Aboriginal and Treaty Rights as well as the Charter of Rights and Freedoms. "Health and safety are at risk when access to safe drinking water is compromised."

The report further states, "This all begs the question, who has responsibility for ensuring the safe provision of drinking water in First Nations communities...? Who is accountable? The lack of clarity in seeking answers to this question was clearly identified in the 2005 Commissioner of Environment and Sustainable Development report as a systemic problem. In 2008, little headway has been made in creating a regulatory regime that could be used to provide needed accountability for ensuring all First Nations have safe drinking water; a key recommendation of the report."

The ongoing issue of First Nations water woes has many causes, but one of them must surely be the issue of overlapping jurisdiction and responsibility. In 2006, an appointed expert panel released a report that gave options for water quality regulation. One of them was to create a regulatory regime through new legislation that would provide the opportunity to set out clearly the roles and responsibilities of all parties involved in providing water and wastewater services on reserves.

The panel said the Constitution Act of 1867 gives the federal government the jurisdiction to develop new federal legislation to govern water on First Nations reserves. But they warned that ensuring safe drinking water involves much more than setting standards and requirements. "In some ways, this is the least important aspect of water system safety. The really critical element is the capacity of facilities and operations to meet the standards."

Only a few exceptional communities have been able to solve the problem of economic resources, which means most other communities have to look to the federal government to meet basic needs, they wrote. "In the area of water and wastewater systems, resources have not been adequate, and the resources made available have not always been used as effectively as they could be."

When it introduced the new Safe Drinking Water for First Nations Act, the federal government said it had committed $2.3 billion between 2006 and 2012 to First Nations water and wastewater infrastructure. During that time, the number of high-risk drinking water systems was reduced from 193 to 49. In addition, out of the 21 communities identified as priorities, which meant that the community had both a high-risk drinking water system and a drinking water advisory, 18 have been removed from the list and action plans are in place for the remaining, it said.

Prairie Provinces Water Management

Canada's three Prairie Provinces have long been watchful of the precious, limited quantity of water that gradually snakes its way through their territories. Alberta had the edge, of course, sitting at the headwaters of the supply, and Saskatchewan and Manitoba worried that without some sort of understanding, their resource could rapidly dwindle to a trickle.

The Apportionment Agreement

The three provinces, together with a federal presence, formed the Prairie Provinces Water Board (PPWB) in 1948 to figure out how to share this interprovincial water. They settled on a method that worked well until the 1960s, when intermittent drought years cranked up the pressure on the water supply. The board found their approach unequal to the task for the kind of long-term water planning necessary for the provinces. A new system of sharing was needed. Finally, in 1969, a master agreement on apportionment was reached. The crux of the new system was the concept of equal sharing. Under the formula, which stands to this day, Alberta is entitled to 50 percent of the natural flow of an interprovincial river before it enters Saskatchewan; Saskatchewan is entitled to 50 percent of the water that enters the province from Alberta and 50 percent of the flow arising within its borders; and Manitoba receives the remainder.

Obviously, figuring out what the "natural flow" is each year is critical to the functioning of the agreement. The parties agreed that natural flow would be defined as the volume of flow that would occur in a particular river if that river had never been affected by human activity. This formula is based on flow occurring over the course of a 12-month period in all eastward flowing streams. "While calculating this amount can be difficult, the result is straightforward—all three provinces, even in drought periods, end up with approximately equal shares of the total water flow," says the board. "It is then solely up to the provinces to decide how they will use their share of water."

Environment Canada steps in to help collect the data used to calculate natural flow. Stream flow is monitored at 14 locations along the Alberta–Saskatchewan and Saskatchewan–Manitoba borders. Although the agreement applies to all eastward flowing interprovincial streams, including those where the water flow is currently not monitored, formal apportionment calculations are only done for eight stream locations with significant water use upstream, the board explains. Other river basins may be added to the monitoring list when water uses in an upstream province become significant. In addition, data that are needed to calculate natural flow are gathered at over 90 sites, located primarily in the South Saskatchewan River and Qu'Appelle River basins.

Environment Canada also collects information on water quality because the 1969 agreement recognized that as an issue as well. In 1992, the parties decided to make the water quality issue official and added a water quality program to their agreement. There is a set of water quality objectives specific to each river reach. Members are supposed to strive to meet these objectives to protect all downstream uses, including aquatic life. When the objectives are not met, a report is prepared, with an explanation and a recommended course of action. The board then makes recommendations to its member agencies on how to resolve any problems.

There is a contingency plan in place to promptly warn downstream water quality management agencies when a spill or some other unusual water condition is detected in an eastward flowing interprovincial stream, or of an event that has the potential to adversely impact interprovincial surface or ground waters.

The last federal report summing up water quality at monitoring stations shows the excellent and good ratings clustering in western Alberta and northern Manitoba, with marginal water being passed on to Saskatchewan from Alberta and fair to marginal water at the Saskatchewan–Manitoba border. It's clear that the big cities and agriculture have an impact. And yet, although concerns do filter into reports, there has been little public political squabbling between the governments so far about water quality issues. The squabbling may be coming, as Manitoba bears the obvious brunt of over-fertilization in Lake Winnipeg and further frets about issues such as the introduction of grass carp in Alberta.

The apportionment agreement has grown deep roots in the Prairie Provinces by now, though. In southern Alberta, and to a lesser extent in southern Saskatchewan, governments and irrigators have invested heavily in dams and other irrigation infrastructure, expanding water use to the limits of their respective apportionments, observes Timothy Heinmiller in a paper published in a 2009 edition of the *International Journal of the Commons*. This investment has created politically powerful vested interests to defend their water use, particularly in Alberta where the Progressive Conservative party has ruled continuously since 1971 based largely on the support of the province's rural ridings, he writes.

"Yet, while the apportionment institution was becoming increasingly entrenched, water conservation issues also began to emerge," writes Heinmiller. As the waters of the Saskatchewan-Nelson basin, which flow from the Rockies through Alberta, Saskatchewan and Manitoba, were increasingly appropriated, water quality deteriorated and some fish stocks went into decline, he says. "By the mid-1980s, the basin's water was so heavily used in its upper reaches that Alberta came close to exceeding its apportionment on the South Saskatchewan River in 1984, 1985 and 1988, and actually exceeded its apportionment on some smaller rivers in a number of years around this time."

The Centre for Hydrology, which is based at the University of Saskatchewan, confirms dry years are a challenge for Alberta, particularly in the South Saskatchewan River. "Overall, Alberta uses 24.5 percent of its natural flows in the South Saskatchewan River," centre scientists wrote in a 2005 report. "In drought years, however, Alberta uses most of its 50 percent apportionment. In the 21st century, changes in precipitation and temperature associated with global warming and increased demand resulting from increases in population will exacerbate water shortages up to the point that availability of clean water will become a key limiting factor to economic and community development in the Prairie Provinces of Canada. As a result, water quantity is a significant and ever-increasing concern in the Prairie Provinces."

But changing the current system to make it more adaptable will be difficult. Heinmiller writes that the established apportionment has proven so resilient that all basin-wide conservation measures have been added to its margins, rather than reforming its core. The water quality objectives added in 1992 are one example. None of the reforms have altered the basic features of the established apportionment institution, and Heinmiller says it remains so influential that it restricts the options for water conservation in the Saskatchewan-Nelson basin.

Northwest Territories Water Management

In the Northwest Territories (NWT), the federal crown may have ownership of the water resources, but that hasn't stopped the territorial government from being very involved in the management of their freshwater resources.

The NWT Water Stewardship Strategy

"Freshwater is fundamental to life," says the first line of the NWT Water Stewardship Strategy, released in the spring of 2010. "Clean and abundant freshwaters ensure healthy, productive ecosystems. These are essential to the social, cultural and economic well-being of people, particularly the residents of the NWT. The rivers, lakes, streams and ponds of the NWT are an essential part of northern life and traditional Aboriginal cultures."

The Government of the Northwest Territories developed the strategy with Indian and Northern Affairs Canada and aboriginal governments to ensure the waters of the NWT remain clean, abundant and productive for all time. "All populations require water to develop and prosper," the strategy acknowledges. But it goes further than that in the NWT. The territory boasts some of the country's largest water features, including the enormous Great Bear Lake—the largest lake found entirely within Canada —and the magnificent Mackenzie River, Canada's longest river at 4241 kilometres long to the head of the Finlay River (the Mackenzie is called *Deh Cho*, or Big River, by the Dene people). There is also Great Slave Lake, Canada's fourth largest lake, and the Mackenzie Delta, the country's largest freshwater delta. Water has shaped the face and culture of the NWT and continues to do so, the document says. "Aboriginal people in the NWT have a long and intimate relationship with the land and water. They draw their spiritual and cultural integrity and their strength from the land and water (i.e., ecosystem)."

Today, residents are concerned about water resources and increasing water-related pressures from development, climate change and a changing global economy, the report says. "Since pressures on waters throughout the NWT and in neighbouring jurisdictions continue to increase, residents have been clear that improved water stewardship is essential."

Michael Miltenberger, the NWT deputy premier, is uneasy about the unseasonably warm 2009–2010 winter—said by Environment Canada to be the country's warmest since nation-wide records began in 1948. He says people are noticing changes to water levels. "We notice the land is changing, water levels are going down in creeks and sloughs. Permafrost is melting. In some places up north, in fact, where the water used to stay because the ground was frozen, once the ground melts the water just disappears." Miltenberger says they have to acknowledge and recognize that the land needs a certain amount of water. "We don't want to be looking like the Colorado, or the Yangtze or the Yellow river, which don't even reach their destinations anymore. They're just sucked dry."

Water quantity is important to northerners. "This land is by definition semi-arid, and without the water it would be desert," Miltenberger says. He's learned that a lot of the water they have is old, so-called "fossil" water—essentially left on the landscape by retreating, melting glaciers from the last ice age.

"The waters of the NWT, both within and outside the Mackenzie River Basin, have many uses," adds the strategy. "They are important for the efficient transport of goods, services and people, both in the winter (ice roads) and summer (barge and other boat traffic). Residents also rely on these waters for personal travel to hunting areas, cultural sites and other communities. Traveling along rivers and lakes by canoe honours and celebrates ties to Aboriginal heritage."

The waters also supply sustenance in the form of fish. But some fish species are disappearing, and the ones that are still around are sometimes deformed or have lesions, Miltenberger says. In the other extreme, salmon are appearing farther north than they've ever been sighted, lured by warmer water.

All of these changes, plus developments happening upstream, such as the oilsands, make people very apprehensive, he says. There have also been some lessons learned from past decisions that show the need for better water stewardship within the NWT, in upstream jurisdictions such as Alberta and British Columbia, and in downstream jurisdictions such as Nunavut, the report says.

Miltenberger gives the example of the now-closed Giant Mine, which has hundreds of thousands of tonnes of poisonous arsenic trioxide crammed into some of its shafts. "It's a huge threat to the water table. If something ever happened and the mine shafts got flooded there would be an enormous downriver pulse of arsenic, killing everything in its path, probably." Dealing with the waste could cost a billion dollars, he says. The Giant Mine is the kind of project that would never get approval today, he adds.

Today, the strategy addresses concerns about upstream developments in neighbouring jurisdictions, which have implications for NWT waters. It specifically names the oilsands operations in northern Alberta. Miltenberger says the thought of a breach in one of the massive oilsands tailings ponds that sits along the Athabasca River is especially unsettling.

Addressing all these water worries is going to be complicated. "We're a territory of 42,000 people," Miltenberger explains. "We've got a territorial government, a federal government and seven aboriginal governments, four of which have land claims settled, three that don't. So that in itself is a fairly sensitive challenge politically." The strategy specifically says it respects aboriginal and treaty rights as well as rights and processes set out in settled lands, resources and self-government agreements.

The federal government has legal authority for the land and water for the most part, he says. The territorial government has been pushing the water strategy solely on the basis of what

Miltenberger describes as their "political and moral authority." So far, the federal government has helped fund a lot of the work done for the strategy, but because of the governance structure, they're going to have to get very involved to help achieve the water security the NWT wants, Miltenberger says.

The Mackenzie River Basin
Transboundary Waters Master Agreement

The process the territory will use to get other jurisdictions to the table is the water management agreements made possible through the Mackenzie River Basin Transboundary Waters Master Agreement, which was signed by the federal government and Alberta, British Columbia, Saskatchewan, Yukon and the NWT. The agreement—which covers over one-sixth of Canada's total area—allows neighbouring jurisdictions to negotiate bilateral water management agreements that address quality, quantity and flow of water on transboundary streams.

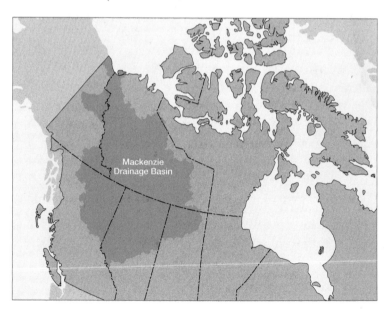

The Mackenzie River Basin Board was set up in 1997 to implement the agreement. The basic goal of the basin board is to make sure there is a healthy and diverse ecosystem in the basin, now and into the future. "It was created and then basically pushed to the side," Miltenberger says. "And the bureaucrats sort of sat there quietly doing stuff for about 12 years until we sort of dragged them back into the light. It's the only process we have to come to the table."

So far, only the NWT and Yukon have signed a bilateral agreement. Once the NWT government is satisfied it has a strong water strategy and all the various parties in the territory agree on what they want, they will begin negotiations with other jurisdictions, Miltenberger says. He doesn't expect those negotiations to be easy. There are "some strong and growing issues" with Alberta and BC, and now with Yukon as well, as they consider development in the Peel River basin. In February 2010, the Yukon government put a one-year moratorium on mineral staking for all lands in the Peel Watershed Region to provide certainty during their ongoing regional land use planning process.

"And political jurisdictions, in Alberta for example, are very, very different than the Northwest Territories. The 60th parallel is a very significant boundary. It's a political line on the map, but the ideologies that govern our approach to the environment are very different." Alberta's politics, in particular, are radically different from the NWT's politics. "They've had a conservative ideology that's permeated from the grassroots right to the highest level. They have a very aggressive development agenda. Their relationship with their aboriginal populations is very different than what they are in the north." BC, on the other hand, just doesn't tend to look north, Miltenberger says. "So it's going to be tough getting their attention."

Negotiations between the NWT and Alberta are expected to begin at the end of 2010 or the beginning of 2011.

Environmental Protection

The federal government uses the Canadian Environmental Assessment Act, proclaimed on January 19, 1995, to express much of its decision-making authority. This act applies whether it's a municipality, a corporation or even some arm of the federal government itself with a project that falls under federal jurisdiction. It affects all projects that require the federal government to fund a project, sell or lease federal lands, or issue permits, licences, grants or approvals. The act is supposed to help identify the possible environmental impacts of each project early in the planning stage. Ultimately, the act is supposed to "encourage responsible authorities to take actions that promote sustainable development and thereby achieve or maintain a healthy environment and a healthy economy."

The potential environmental impacts are identified and described by experts, whether they be qualified biologists, chemists, engineers and so forth. Local people in the area also have the opportunity to submit their concerns about a project to the review panel appointed to weigh all the input on a particular project.

Wetlands

Wetlands are a frequent subject of environmental assessments under the act. While wetland conservation is a shared responsibility of the provinces and territories and the federal government, federal responsibilities include maintaining the quality of the environment, migratory bird populations, inland and ocean fisheries and international or transboundary resources such as water and wildlife.

The federal government says it considers Canada's wetlands —29 percent of which are on federal lands or waters—as integral to sustainable development and environmental quality. Says the Canadian Environmental Assessment Agency (CEAA), which administers the act for which it is named:

Wetlands perform important ecological functions that sustain the quality of land, water and air. For example, wetlands filter and purify water. They control floods, recharge groundwater supplies, augment summer water flows and reduce erosion. Wetlands provide habitat for more than 600 wildlife species in North America, and one-third of Canada's species at risk depend on wetlands for their survival. Communities depend on wetlands for food, recreation and commercial activities such as fishing. Wetlands also store carbon; current studies are looking into their potential role as a carbon sink in the context of climate change.

Consequently, the loss or degradation of wetlands to development means substantial and far-reaching costs to the environment, to wildlife and to people—costs that should be considered as legitimate 'environmental effects' but that are rarely given enough weight in EA decisions.

The agency quotes Robert Costanza, an ecological economics expert at the University of Maryland, who estimated the economic value of ecological services performed by wetlands. These services include water regulation, water supply, erosion control, waste treatment, wildlife habitat, food production and recreation. "Costanza's conclusions reinforce the enormous ecological benefits of wetlands compared to other types of ecosystems," the agency says. "Wetlands are valued at more than C$22,000 per hectare per year for the ecological functions they provide. In contrast, forests, grasslands and croplands are worth a fraction of this value. The only systems valued higher than terrestrial wetlands are estuaries, valued at C$34,000 per hectare per year, and seagrass algae beds, valued at over C$28,000 per hectare per year—and a good portion of estuaries and seagrass beds also constitute 'wetlands' within the Canadian definition."

The Federal Policy on Wetland Conservation was adopted in the early 1990s with the goal of halting substantial losses of these valuable ecosystems. The central goal of the policy is "no net loss." Basically, this means that there should be no overall loss of wetlands on the landscape. It would be best if wetlands were not impacted at all by development, but if it can't be avoided then the next best goal is to minimize the damage as much as possible. And as a last resort, compensation comes into play. This means replacing unavoidably lost wetland functions by enhancing or rehabilitating existing wetlands or creating new wetlands.

Canada has more than 127 million hectares of wetlands, which add up to 24 percent of the world's wetland area. In addition to efforts between federal and provincial jurisdictions, the federal government has also signed onto international agreements. One such agreement is the Ramsar Convention on Wetlands, signed in Iran in 1971. Canada signed the convention in 1981, pledging to use wetlands wisely by designating these specific areas to protect them for Canadians and the rest of the world.

Since then, 37 of Canada's wetlands have been designated as Ramsar sites, totalling more than 13 million hectares and representing eight percent of the total wetland area in Canada. The sites include the Columbia Wetlands, which provide nesting and rearing habitat for over 180 species of birds; the vast tundra plains of the Queen Maud Gulf Migratory Bird Sanctuary in Nunavut; and the extraordinary Cap Tourmente National Wildlife Area, where coastal marshes and snow geese are enjoyed by about 100,000 visitors every year, says a 2008 report on the sites.

The survey of managers of all these sites reported some problems, though. Managers of 15 of the 37 sites report changes in the ecological character of the wetland since designation as a Ramsar site, the 2008 report says. At one of the sites, the designated lake has virtually disappeared. Other managers reported reduced ecological diversity and habitat degradation due to a boom in snow geese, increased numbers of invasive species, algal blooms and increased off-highway vehicle use. But most of the site managers who reported changes said the Ramsar designation helped maintain the ecological character of the site, implying the changes in the ecological character of these important wetlands may have been greater in the absence of the Ramsar designation.

More generally, Ducks Unlimited says as much as 70 percent of Canada's original wetlands have been lost in some areas of the country. "Canada cannot afford to lose more," the organization says. "Wetlands naturally filter our water and provide habitat for approximately 600 wildlife species."

Ducks Unlimited is heavily involved in another federal wetlands commitment, called the North American Waterfowl Management Plan. It was signed by Canada and the United States in 1986 and by Mexico in 1994. In its 2009 progress report, the Canadian plan administrators say they have secured 2.9 million hectares of important wetlands and associated upland habitat, taking them to 86 percent of their goal. Ultimately, this secured habitat is meant to return waterfowl populations to their 1970s levels. This work is done through joint ventures, involving public agencies and private organizations, such as Ducks Unlimited, the Nature Conservancy and dozens of other agencies, corporations and government departments.

Freshwater Ecosystems

One way of judging the effectiveness of governance in environmental protection is by looking at the parade of imperilled species dependent on freshwater ecosystems.

Canada has relatively low species diversity when it comes to freshwater fish. A 2008 paper in *BioScience* referred to 13,400 freshwater fish species worldwide, but said each year new species are being discovered—as many as four per day in places like South America. McGill University scientists say Canada has fewer than 200 of those freshwater species. They say this is largely due to glaciers, which scour the country clean of fish wherever they advance during ice ages. The fish slowly find their way back between glaciations. Compare Canada to Lake Victoria, which straddles Uganda, Kenya and Tanzania, and was once home to 500 freshwater fish species.

Nationally, the Committee on the Status of Endangered Wildlife in Canada (COSEWIC) monitors the health of plant and animal populations and provides recommendations to the government on whether or not a species should be designated as endangered, threatened or otherwise. As of the end of 2009, there were 598 plants and animals assessed in various risk categories, including 250 endangered, 150 threatened, 162 special concern and 23 extirpated (i.e. no longer found in the wild in Canada). So far, 13 wildlife species are extinct. Almost half of the extinct species —six—are freshwater fish.

Freshwater Fish That Have Gone Extinct

Species	Extinction date	Range of occurrence
Deepwater cisco	1952	Ontario
Lake Ontario kiyi	1964	Ontario
Blue walleye	1965	Ontario
Banff longnose dace	1986	Alberta
Benthic Hadley Lake stickleback	1999	British Columbia
Limnetic Hadley Lake stickleback	1999	British Columbia

What makes freshwater fish so vulnerable? Some of them have very limited habitat—or at least they did by the time we found them. The two Hadley Lake stickleback species, for example, were only known to inhabit that lake, located on Lasqueti Island. They were lost as a result of nest predation by the illegally introduced brown bullhead catfish.

The Banff longnose dace was found only in Banff National Park, in a marsh into which the Cave and Basin Hotsprings drain, according to The Canadian Biodiversity Web Site maintained by

McGill University. The site says there is no estimate for the past size of the population. COSEWIC says the longnose dace was lost as a result of competition with introduced exotic fishes, habitat alteration and degradation (leakage of chlorine from a swimming pool into the marsh and construction of a beaver dam) and hybridization with a similar subspecies.

The other three species—blue walleye, deepwater cisco and Lake Ontario kiyi—were driven to extinction by over-exploitation, much of which occurred earlier in the 20th century.

There are similar stories in COSEWIC's extirpated category, where four fish find themselves. The striped bass population from the St. Lawrence Estuary disappeared as a consequence of illegal fishing, with the last record dating from 1968.

The historic Canadian range of a small minnow called the gravel chub was originally a single watershed in southern Ontario. The last record for this species was in 1958, despite extensive, repeated sampling at known sites and other areas of suitable habitat over the last 50 years. COSEWIC says ecosystem restoration of this watershed is underway, but the fish won't come back on its own because there are no adjacent populations in the Great Lakes watershed.

The paddlefish was also once found in the Great Lakes, but was apparently never common in the Canadian portion of its range. It has not been observed in Canadian waters since 1917, despite extensive sampling and the fact that such a distinctive fish would have been easily recognizable. Yes, it has a paddle-like extension sticking out far beyond its snout.

Paddlefish *(Polyodon spathula)*

Atlantic salmon was once a prolific species throughout the Lake Ontario watershed, but there has been no record of this fish in the lake since 1898. Again, the species was extinguished through habitat destruction and through over-exploitation by the food and commercial fishery, COSEWIC explains. Attempts to reestablish Atlantic salmon through stocking have failed, and the original strain is no longer available.

Biologists Jeffrey Hutchings and Marco Festa-Bianchet published a study in 2009 that looked at how species are assessed and listed. The current and past chairmen of COSEWIC took a particular interest in fish species. They found that from April 1978 through December 2008, one-fifth of assessments done by COSEWIC were for fish species. Three-quarters of the fish assessed were either freshwater or diadromous, which means they migrate between fresh and salt water. The remainder were marine species. "Slightly more than one-quarter (27 percent) of Canada's 205 freshwater and diadromous species of fishes, many of which are in southwestern Ontario and southeastern Quebec, have been assessed as being at risk throughout all or parts of their ranges," they wrote. During the first 20 years of assessments, most fish ended up in the special concern category, they noted. The situation is worsening, though. Since the late 1990s, most species have been assessed as endangered.

During the first decade of fish assessments, the species considered were concentrated in southwestern Ontario. The distribution expanded during the first 20 years of assessments to include more of southern British Columbia and southern Quebec, with the density of species at risk most noticeably increasing in southern Ontario, Quebec and Manitoba. Summarizing all assessments from 1980 through 2008, the distribution of fish species at risk has increased across the country, with the highest concentrations in southern British Columbia, southern Manitoba, southwestern Ontario and southeastern Quebec.

Fish are not the only animals associated with freshwater ecosystems that are suffering. The tiger salamander once lived in the Canadian portion of the Great Lakes basin. It was last seen in southern Ontario in 1915 at Point Pelee. Despite repeated inventories over the last 80 years, it has not been seen since that time. It is also endangered in BC, as is the small-mouthed salamander in Ontario.

Another victim of change is the dwarf wedgemussel. Formerly found in New Brunswick, the species hasn't been seen in Canada since 1968. It is a freshwater mussel that lives in everything from streams to deep rivers. The only recorded Canadian location for the dwarf wedgemussel is the Petitcodiac River drainage of New Brunswick, says the McGill website. A specimen was last collected there in 1960, at which time the species was classified as being common. It became extirpated in 1968, following construction of a causeway. It is considered endangered in the Atlantic states where it can still be found.

Even something as small as Bert's predaceous diving beetle is having trouble holding its niche and finds itself on the endangered list. This Canadian endemic species is known from only two locations in southern Alberta, one of which has been destroyed, COSEWIC says. It is limited to springs and seepage areas along steep cliff edges or river bends. Its habitat is declining due to trampling by livestock and lowering of the water table due to withdrawals for irrigation.

Four species of frog are on the endangered list, too. So are the five-lined skink, various turtles, the Lake Erie watersnake and the bogbean buckmoth. And on it goes.

Under the Species At Risk Act (SARA), which came into force in 2003, the federal government is supposed to work together with the provincial and territorial ministers responsible for wildlife to protect species at risk. The goal is to prevent species in Canada from becoming extinct as a consequence of human activity.

But environmental groups have successfully taken the federal government to court over its failure to protect species. In 2007, Ecojustice filed a lawsuit on behalf of environmental groups against the federal Minister of Fisheries and Oceans for refusing to identify critical habitat for the Nooksack dace, an endangered fish that lives in small streams in BC's Fraser Valley, east of Vancouver. SARA specifically requires critical habitat to be identified as part of the action plan to save a species. "Despite this requirement, officials with the Department of Fisheries and Oceans removed specific sections from a draft version of the recovery strategy identifying the critical habitat of the Nooksack dace," Ecojustice said.

Members of the government-appointed Nooksack dace scientific recovery team also spoke out about the critical habitat decision, saying that the government had done the same thing to other endangered species across the country and that this instance was a systemic failure.

More than 80 percent of species listed under SARA are endangered primarily because of habitat loss or destruction, Ecojustice pointed out, and the Nooksack dace was no exception. Gravel mining, agricultural drainage, urban sprawl and the depletion of streams for farm irrigation and residential use had all harmed the habitat of the once-abundant dace.

In 2009, the federal court agreed with Ecojustice. Justice Douglas Campbell ruled that the Department of Fisheries and Oceans has been using an unlawful policy direction. Incredibly, that policy directed that critical habitat should be removed from all recovery strategies for all aquatic species in BC. It appeared that the DFO had applied its unlawful policy to at least 20 other species in the province, Ecojustice said. Recovery strategies for those species now need to be rewritten. The environmental groups now hope that the federal government will protect species the way it's supposed to, instead of having to be dragged to court for every case.

CHAPTER FIVE

Provincial Water Governance

PROVINCES TAKE OVER WATER governance for bodies of water that lie solely within their boundaries. As mentioned earlier, Yukon also manages its own water resources, while Indian and Northern Affairs Canada manages those of Nunavut and the Northwest Territories. The provinces also have legislative powers over water supply, flow regulation, authorization of water use development, and thermal and hydroelectric power development.

The provinces tend to delegate most of the water portfolio to their environment and natural resources ministries, but there are some exceptions. Saskatchewan has a specific Crown water utility service provider, which delivers drinking water and takes care of wastewater treatment services for Saskatchewan municipalities, industry and rural water user groups. And Manitoba has a separate water stewardship department charged with protecting the social, economic and environmental values of water.

Water Standards

Although the federal government provides guidance on what drinking water should and should not contain through the Canadian Drinking Water Guidelines, it's really up to the provinces to follow through. David Schindler has a problem with this. "We have national water quality guidelines in this country and nobody pays attention to them, which is part of the problem," he says. "Guidelines aren't legally enforceable. So if you break a guideline there's nothing they can do except say to you, 'See, you've broken a guideline. You better go back and see if you can get your water quality back up.' [Whereas with] a standard, the government can immediately take you to court for going over."

Schindler would prefer to see well-crafted, legislated national guidelines on all kinds of water issues. Because otherwise, he says, "…we've got this hodgepodge of rules that vary from province to province."

The Program on Water Governance, based at the University of British Columbia, confirms there is huge variation in the management of drinking water across Canada. Alberta and Nova Scotia are the only regions to have fully adopted the national guidelines in binding legislation, the program says.

The laissez-faire attitude to drinking water guidelines punches some significant holes in the multi-barrier approach to providing safe water. A key barrier is, of course, water treatment, which includes disinfection and filtration. But less than half of Canada's jurisdictions have filtration policies to remove contaminants and microorganisms, says the Program on Water Governance, based on a 2007 survey. (Those provinces are Ontario, Alberta, Saskatchewan, Nova Scotia and Quebec.) The U.S. has legislation that has required filtration of surface water since 1989, the program says.

Many provinces and territories have moved to modernize their water legislation in the last decade following the Walkerton and North Battleford fiascos and the increasing pressures of development and climate change. Rob de Loë considers this movement a source of considerable hope. All across the country, almost without exception, provincial governments have recognized the significance of water, he says. A decade ago, the situation was reversed. For the most part, water was simply not a priority. De Loë says it would be nice to pin the blame for that indifference on somebody, but he feels that we "all somehow came to this silent consensus, that water wasn't terribly important."

In Ontario, it took the deaths of people in Walkerton to shock the system and cause the fundamental rethink that we're seeing today, he adds. "Walkerton rippled across the country, and the fact that North Battleford happened shortly thereafter was another wake-up call."

But the factors spurring provincial reforms were more numerous than those two disasters. In Alberta, the process of changing the Water Act began in the 1990s, long before Walkerton. Scarcity was one reason. "I would say Alberta is ground zero in Canada for water scarcity at the regional or provincial scale," de Loë says. "Nobody else is in as tight shape as Alberta." But every province has faced its own awakening, he adds. "In Prince Edward Island, for example, they had to stop giving new licences for high capacity irrigation wells because they're 100 percent groundwater dependent, and they realized, 'Whoa Nelly, we don't really know where we're going with this so we have to slow down.' In Quebec, water quality concerns were important."

Water Rights

FITFIR: First in Time, First in Right

The provinces have different ways of assigning water rights. In BC, Alberta, Saskatchewan and Manitoba, a system called "first in time, first in right" has been used for over 100 years now. Commonly called FITFIR (pronounced "fit-fur") the approach uses seniority to decide who gets water during shortages. The senior licence holders, the ones who got their licences first, have first dibs on the water. Until recently, these licences were also issued "in perpetuity," and maximum water use was encouraged by a use-it-or-lose-it rule.

Some provinces have begun tinkering with this approach, or outright bailing on it. Saskatchewan no longer uses it, and BC recognizes that allocating water in perpetuity provides few incentives for water users to be efficient. "It is argued that this practice contributes to BC being one of the largest per capita water users in the world," the government says. The FITFIR system was designed for a time when water shortages were uncommon, but pressures have changed, and like elsewhere, weaknesses have emerged, the province adds. "The system needs to be more efficient, flexible, and capable of adapting to changing conditions, particularly as pressures on water supplies intensify and supply patterns change."

BC is currently working on a new water strategy called Living Water Smart. The government says modifications to the FITFIR system "could range from small incremental modifications to major shifts." New legislation to modernize the Water Act is taking longer than expected, with the government announcing it would allow comments on specific modernization proposals in late 2010.

In Manitoba, the system has a few caveats. The province's Water Rights Act says that when licences are issued on an identical date, a priority system takes effect, placing domestic and municipal needs above agricultural, industrial and irrigation needs, in that order. The government also has the power to suspend or restrict licence rights if science tells them there is not enough water to protect aquatic ecosystems.

Alberta, meanwhile, has stuck to FITFIR, maintaining it through the rewrite of its Water Act in 1999. The revision allows for water rights to be transferred, though. These transfers must be authorized in approved water management plans or by order of the Lieutenant Governor in Council.

The FITFIR system has come under heavy fire in Alberta, with critics saying the system is highly inappropriate in a province facing population and industrial growth in tandem with increasing water scarcity. Even the province's former environment minister, Lorne Taylor, thinks the system is outdated. "First-in-time, first-in-right is not unique to Alberta, but it is a policy that has served its purpose and time," he wrote in a 2009 edition of *Policy Options*, a Canadian public policy magazine. "In light of the current state of Alberta's water supplies, it is no longer an appropriate water management policy."

The government of Alberta is reviewing its current water allocation management system "with a mindset to adapt and respond to today's regional water needs," it says. No timeline has been set for a completion of the review.

Riparian Rights and Civil Code

Other forms of water rights rules used in Canada include riparian rights and civil code. Riparian rights are used to govern, in part, water allocation in Ontario and the Maritimes. This is an old system adopted from England that bestows water rights to a landowner who happens to live next to a water source. The landowner can use the water for household purposes. Additionally, water for irrigation or manufacture on the land is permitted as long as the water is returned to its source in similar quantity and quality after use, says the Program on Water Governance, which has studied water rights across the country. The program notes that riparian rights apply to surface water, not groundwater, and that in Ontario, permits are required for withdrawals of more than 50,000 litres per day for industrial uses or bottling.

Next door, the Civil Code of Québec establishes the use of all surface and groundwater resources as "common to all." The province passed a new water resources protection act in the summer of 2009. It confirms the legal status of both surface water and groundwater as collective resources that are "part of the common heritage of the Québec nation." It recognizes the right of every person to have access to safe drinking water and sets out certain principles, including the duty to prevent damage to water resources and repair any such damage.

The act also established a new water withdrawal authorization system that gives priority to satisfying the needs of the population but also reconciles ecosystem needs and the needs of economic activities. The term of water withdrawal authorizations is 10 years, unless otherwise determined. The province also has the power to reduce or stop a water withdrawal that presents a serious risk to public health or aquatic ecosystems.

Dams and Diversions

One of the most significant powers held by the provinces is their jurisdiction over dam building and diversions. Not only can dams and diversions affect water supply in a province during the course of a year, but they also can have a great influence over the supply and price of electricity.

Dams

Dams help produce hydroelectricity, which is created when water moves a turbine connected to an electrical generator. The higher a dam is the more power it can produce, since the falling water provides the driving force that makes the turbine blades spin. The volume of water is obviously also important.

Hydropower is one of the most efficient sources of energy. Modern hydropower stations can convert more than 95 percent of the available energy in the river into electricity, while the best fossil fuel power plants, the combined cycle cogeneration plants, are only about 60 percent efficient, according to the Canadian Hydropower Association. Canada's adoption of hydroelectric power sources goes back to at least 1881, when a water wheel at

Chaudière Falls on the Ottawa River produced electricity that was used to power streetlights and local mills in Ottawa. As of 2008, Canada produced almost 12 percent of the world's hydroelectricity, second only to China. Hydroelectricity accounts for approximately 60 percent of Canada's electricity production, the association says.

But dams have some damaging effects, too. Many dams are associated with reservoirs, which are artificial lakes created when a dam is built across a river, blocking the flow of water. This action can blunt or completely eliminate the natural flooding cycle of the river downstream of the dam, a consequence that many biologists and environmentalists decry as harmful to ecosystems. For example, cottonwoods in southern Alberta rely on the floods to provide them with barren sand bars bereft of competitors. Flooding is also a mechanism by which rivers deposit nutrients. In the reservoir, toxic metals such as mercury build up. And though hydropower is often touted for its ability to produce electricity without greenhouse gases, reservoirs do produce some emissions as vegetation decomposes. In the U.S., more than 700 dams have been removed in recent years for various reasons, ranging from reducing flood risks to restoring vital aquatic ecosystems. Whether or not Canada will follow suit remains to be seen.

The Canadian Dam Association has 933 large dams (higher than 15 metres) registered. Thousands more small dams exist. Although construction of dams as a whole seems to have declined since the 1970s, there are still large projects on the books, so it's unclear if Canada has yet passed its major period of large dam building, says an Environment Canada analysis. Canada ranks as one of the world's top 10 dam builders, according to Environment Canada.

Quebec has clearly embraced the technology, having built one-third of the country's large dams. The abundance of hydropower generated by the provincial utility Hydro-Quebec keeps electricity prices low and delivers fat dividends to its sole shareholder, the provincial government. Montreal citizens paid the lowest average residential prices among large cities in Canada in 2009, according to a Hydro-Quebec report. The utility has plans to expand, with 1000 megawatts to come online in 2013 and 1550 megawatts by 2020. The company will unveil another 3000 megawatts of major hydropower projects in a future strategic plan. In addition, the province has a stunning 44,100 megawatts of undeveloped hydropower potential, according to a 2006 report.

The three jurisdictions with the next greatest potential are BC, Yukon and Alberta. Yukon has left its potential largely untapped, but so far its four large dams fill the bulk of the territory's electricity needs. Other provinces with many large dams are Ontario, BC and Newfoundland and Labrador. Those three combined don't top Quebec's total by much, though.

Not all of Canada's dams rely on reservoirs. Instead of storing water, run-of-river projects produce power by partially diverting fast-flowing rivers through a turbine set in the river or off to the side. Of 475 hydroelectricity generating stations in Canada, more than 125 are run-of-river, the Canadian Hydropower Association says.

Small hydropower is also favoured to become a bigger player in Canada's energy profile, with less than one-third of the nation-wide potential of 15,000 megawatts developed. CanmetENERGY, the clean energy research arm of Natural Resources Canada, is testing new "fish-friendly" turbines for small generators that are supposed to minimize the risk of injury or death for the many fish in our rivers.

While about 65 percent of Canada's large dams are built to generate hydroelectricity, the remainder have a variety of uses that include providing a water supply, irrigation, flood control and recreation. Another 82 dams store tailings, the waste product of various types of mining. Canada's largest dam, and one of the largest in the world, is actually an oilsands tailings dam built by Syncrude. About 540 million cubic metres of mine tailings were used in its construction. The U.S. Department of the Interior, which compares its Hoover Dam against other dams, ranked the Syncrude dam number one by volume of construction material. It noted the dam is likely to continue its growth as the company continues to mine.

Diversions

Also under provincial authority is the right to divert water from its natural course. This ancient practice plays a key role in irrigation. In Alberta, which soaked up 73% of all irrigation water used in the country in 2007, irrigation districts are allowed to pull up to 2.8 million acre-feet of water out of the local rivers, which works out to about 3.4 trillion litres. Granted, the districts don't use the full amount. However, Alberta's southern basins are over-allocated. In 2006, the province announced it wouldn't be accepting new water licence applications for the most southerly river basins: the Bow, the Oldman and the South Saskatchewan.

Unlike irrigation diversions, which tend to be intra-basin transfers, hydroelectric projects can involve moving water from one river basin to another. This practice is called an interbasin transfer.

Manitoba Hydro has permission to divert up to 850 cubic metres per second from the Churchill River into the Nelson River. The utility admits there have been environmental impacts, including flooding of forested areas and marshes that has affected the livelihoods of trappers and commercial fishers. As of 2008, the company had paid out $290 million in compensation.

Another enormous diversion in Canada dates back to the days of World War II. In a historical note written about the DeCew Falls development, Ontario Power Generation writes that "the setbacks, including the fall of France, which were experienced during the early years of the war, made it evident that the war might last much longer, that Canada would be called upon to speed up the production of munitions and undertake many new industrial tasks, and that as a result the large actual and potential reserves of power which the Hydro-Electric Power Commission of Ontario had available at the outbreak of war might not be sufficient should the war last until 1943 or 1944."

Great Lakes Diversions

To produce more power at a station near St. Catharines, Ontario, an existing diversion at Long Lac that poured water into Lake Superior was combined with a new diversion project built at the Ogoki River. Construction began in November 1940 and was completed and officially opened on July 20, 1943. The project diverts almost all of the flow from the Ogoki River above Waboose Rapids from the Albany River watershed. A 15-metre-high, half-kilometre-long concrete dam at Waboose Rapids holds back the water, and this dam, together with the nearby Summit Control dam and a number of earth-fill side dams, creates a 259-square-kilometre reservoir. Eventually, the water makes its way into Lake Nipigon and then streams via the Nipigon River into Lake Superior. The diverted water amounts to about 113 cubic metres per second, the utility says.

This diversion redirects a massive amount of water into the Great Lakes basin that would have flowed to Hudson Bay. In a 2000 report, the International Joint Commission said more water is diverted into the Great Lakes basin through the Long Lac and Ogoki diversions than is diverted out of the basin at

Chicago and by several small diversions in the United States. "If the Long Lac and Ogoki diversions were not in place, water levels would be 6 centimetres lower in Lake Superior, 11 centimetres lower in Lakes Michigan-Huron, 8 centimetres lower in Lake Erie, and 7 centimetres lower in Lake Ontario."

James Bay Project – Rupert River Diversion

Adapted from Brian Back/Ottertooth.com

The James Bay Project in Quebec is another colossal undertaking. It involved diverting the Eastmain, Opinaca and Caniapiscau rivers to the La Grande River, doubling its average annual flow. The land-claims settlement involved in the project included payments of $225 million to the Cree, Inuit and Naskapis communities in the area. The La Grande hydroelectric complex consists of nine generating stations and required the impounding of reservoirs with a total area of 13,577 square kilometres. The generating stations' total installed capacity is about 16,000 megawatts. The company is now expanding the project by diverting water from the Rupert River, as well.

Quebec obviously isn't swimming in the same direction as the federal government, which claims environmental and social considerations are making interbasin diversions a less desirable option and that "it is widely recognized that we have moved away from the era of large scale diversions and transfers in Canada and the United States." The current approach favours reducing the demand on water uses, Environment Canada says.

Municipal Involvement

Whatever the rules provincially, the municipalities usually end up running the water systems. Municipalities have water rights delegated to them by provincial governments. Often they take care of drinking water treatment and distribution and wastewater treatment operations. In more rural areas, this responsibility is often undertaken by co-operatives of several counties or rural districts.

The municipalities attempt to build and staff systems themselves that will comply with the rules of their provincial overlords. As we've seen earlier, they don't always succeed. Sometimes the municipality will get some help from the private sector in a public-private partnership, or P3. Complete privatization of water services in Canada has so far been met with public distrust and disfavour.

Governance of the Great Lakes and Other International Waters

IN THE MID-1990S, I ventured from a prairie province dotted with murky lakes to a small cabin on a sandspit that juts about 40 kilometres into Lake Erie. Never before had that much water surrounded me—it felt like I was on an island. I might as well have been, because the Long Point Bird Observatory where I was volunteering was accessible only by boat. The cabin where we were housed was located not far from the lighthouse near the very end of the sandspit. This delicate finger of sand seemed ill-equipped to fend off the strong winds and waves that buffeted the peninsula. I was amazed that the migration monitoring station hadn't yet been dragged away by the lake in one of its stormier moods.

Tempestuous Lake Erie has inflicted plenty of damage in its time. The lake is shallow and easily roused by winds into waves reaching several metres high. There are at least 200 shipwrecks around Long Point alone. Observatory staff never attempted a resupply boat trip to the aptly named Tip station without first listening to lake condition forecasts. And this was just Lake Erie, which has the smallest volume of the Great Lakes.

Despite their might, though, these massive bodies of water have proven vulnerable to the overwhelming influence of the 40 million humans living in their watersheds. The lakes have suffered many ills since we settled their shores. In the late 1960s and early 1970s, algal blooms coated and thickened Lake Erie and Lake Ontario to a pea soup–like appearance and consistency. Lake Erie, it was commented, was "too thick to flow and too thin to plow." The surfeit of phosphorus that prompted the blooms wasn't the only problem plaguing the lakes. PCBs, DDT and other chemicals climbed the Great Lakes food chains, decimating populations of top predators such as bald eagles. It is a testament to the cumulative power of the human species that we can so thoroughly contaminate that 20 percent of the world's freshwater contained within the Great Lakes.

These were not problems that Canadians alone could solve. The Great Lakes remain a prime example of the need for international cooperation. After all, molecules of "Canadian" water mix with molecules of "American" water throughout the Great Lakes basin. Water in the basin exists in a kind of conveyor belt, pushed by gravity down an elevation gradient from Lake Superior and Lake Michigan to Lake Huron. From there, water flows to Lake Erie, to Lake Ontario and finally into the St. Lawrence Seaway. Being the superb solvent that it is, water will carry any number of contaminants down the line. Aside from the inter-lake sharing, each lake has its own watershed that contributes water, sediments and chemicals. In the 1960s, it was clear that a couple of the lakes were suffering from pollution, however it got there. So Canada and the United States approached the International Joint Commission (IJC) to look into the issue and report back on it as soon as possible.

The International Joint Commission

The International Joint Commission (IJC) is a creature of the Boundary Waters Treaty, which was signed in 1909. The commission deals with issues concerning boundary waters, defined in the treaty as "the waters from main shore to main shore of the lakes and rivers and connecting waterways, or the portions thereof, along which the international boundary between the United States and the Dominion of Canada passes, including all bays, arms, and inlets thereof, but not including tributary waters which in their natural channels would flow into such lakes, rivers, and waterways, or waters flowing from such lakes, rivers, and waterways, or the waters of rivers flowing across the boundary."

Canada and the U.S. realized early on that what each of them did in the rivers and lakes they shared along the border could affect the other. It was in their interests to work together to protect the shared resource that, among other functions, is used to irrigate crops, provide drinking water and generate hydroelectric power. "These differing needs conflict from time to time," the commission says. And so it steps in, authorizing uses while protecting competing interests.

The first meeting of the IJC took place in 1912 (it took that much time from 1909 to adopt necessary legislation and appoint the first commissioners). Since then, the Boundary Waters Treaty has helped Canada and the U.S. sort out their skirmishes regarding water issues along an 8800-kilometre border. Each side has three members on the commission, which sets up boards to help it sort through issues.

The International Joint Commission's work can be summed in three roles:

Administrative: it administers water apportionment arrangements agreed to under the Boundary Waters Treaty

Regulatory: its approval is required for any work in boundary waters affecting water levels on either side of the boundary

Investigative: it studies, reports and makes recommendations on issues referred to it by the Canadian and American governments.

The types of issues the IJC has dealt with include the construction of dams and canals. If it approves a project, the commission can set conditions limiting water levels and flows to protect shore properties and wetlands and the interests of farmers, shippers and others. After the structure is built, the commission may continue to play a role in how it is operated. Pollution problems, like those seen in Lake Erie and Lake Ontario in the 1960s, are also investigated.

Canada – United States Transboundary Basins

A drainage basin is an area that drains all precipitation received as a runoff or base flow (groundwater sources) into a particular river or set of rivers. Canada's major drainage regions are the Atlantic Ocean, Hudson Bay, Arctic Ocean, Pacific Ocean and Gulf of Mexico.

As the map shows, the IJC's scope extends far beyond the Great Lakes–St. Lawrence River system, though much of its attention is focused there. The commission says it has continuing responsibilities in several other areas. "In the west, the commission has established conditions for dams on the Kootenay, Osoyoos and Columbia rivers, which cross through the states of Washington, Idaho and Montana, and the province of British Columbia. The commission has also helped to set rules for sharing the St. Mary and Milk rivers in Alberta, Saskatchewan and Montana. In the mid-west, the commission has been involved in how the Souris River is shared among Saskatchewan, Manitoba and North Dakota. It also sets emergency water levels for the Rainy Lake system, which crosses through Minnesota, Manitoba and western Ontario, and has helped protect water quality in the Rainy River. In the east, the commission plays a role in regulating dams on the St. Croix River, which flows through New Brunswick and Maine, and in protecting the quality of the river."

IJC Track Record

The track record of the Boundary Waters Treaty and the IJC over the years serves as an illustrative list of the evolution of our scientific and political understanding of water issues.

One early success involved a health issue. In the early 1900s, an IJC investigation helped communities learn more about bacterial pollution in their area. The discharge of sewage and manufacturing wastes had led to outbreaks of cholera and other serious problems. Today, annual cases of cholera have dwindled to single digits in Canada, and they're contracted while visiting other countries.

One of the first disputes the IJC dealt with was a fight over the water from the St. Mary River. Farmers in Montana dug a canal to divert water from the St. Mary River to the Milk River. In response, Alberta farmers started to dig a canal of their own to divert the water back. The Boundary Waters Treaty settled the dispute by divvying up the combined flow from the two rivers equally between the countries. The IJC then developed an apportionment regime to carry out the treaty provisions.

The issue has come full circle now after being re-opened in 2003 at the request of Montana's governor. Alberta and Montana now want to "improve the timing and access to this shared water." A 12-member team of local water users and government officials from both sides of the border is exploring options and is supposed to issue a report with joint recommendations in late 2010.

Old Man River Basin and Milk River Basin

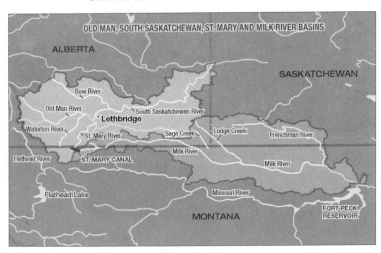

The Columbia River, which flows from British Columbia down to the Pacific Ocean through the U.S., was also once a source of potential conflict. In the mid-1940s, the IJC completed a major study of the water resources in the Columbia River basin, which it says set the stage for coordinated development. This basin extends through much of Washington, Oregon, Idaho and

Montana and even dips into Wyoming, Utah and Nevada, so its importance could not be overestimated.

Columbia River Basin

The IJC's recommended principles for sharing flood control and electric power benefits helped the two federal governments negotiate the Columbia River Treaty, signed in 1961 and activated in until 1964. The deal addressed dams, hydropower, water storage and flood control. The treaty does not expire, but may be renewed, terminated or renegotiated in 2024 if either country gives notice in 2014, the commission says. The Columbia River has 14 major dams on it, three in BC. Since the treaty was signed, populations of salmon that spawn in the river have plunged, and critics say the treaty needs to be renegotiated to accommodate endangered wildlife and the pressures of climate change.

The same sort of pressure to reopen old agreements hit the Lake Ontario–St. Lawrence River area in the mid-1990s. In 1952, the IJC had approved a major hydroelectric power project in the region based on flow levels it set to reduce flooding to shoreline communities, improve commercial shipping and generate electricity. In 1999, the commission said there was a need to more fully consider environmental factors, which were poorly understood when the current orders of approval were issued in the 1950s. As a result, the commission added, it was launching an action plan to review the regulation of flows set for the Moses-Saunders Dam between Massena, New York, and Cornwall, Ontario. Recreational boating had also developed in the region, and the effects of climate change and variability needed to be taken into account. It's been a slow process, though. As of May 2010, a working group had received, at its third meeting, some expert analysis on scientific and technical issues related to regulating the levels and flow of water from Lake Ontario into the St. Lawrence River.

The IJC has also smoothed the way for work on water quality in the Great Lakes basin. The first Great Lakes Water Quality Agreement was signed in 1972. The deal was that each country would work to control pollution and clean up industrial and municipal wastewaters. But as science sniffed out new problems with synthetic chemicals, the need to keep them out of the Great Lakes grew. A new agreement was signed in 1978, shifting the focus to "persistent toxic substances" such as DDT and PCBs.

"The most profound new feature of the 1978 Agreement was the call for an ecosystem approach to management, making ecological integrity rather than only water chemistry the accepted goal of the Great Lakes community," noted Lee Botts and Paul Muldoon in a 1996 study on the water quality agreements. The next phase of the agreement, from 1978 to the addition of a new protocol in 1987, was dominated by confirmation of the complexity and seriousness of toxic contamination of the ecosystem and by growing public concern, but also by confusion and uncertainty about how this problem could be managed, they added.

The 1987 protocol amended the 1978 agreement, aiming to strengthen the programs and increase accountability for their implementation. New goals included addressing atmospheric deposition of toxic pollutants, contaminated sediments and groundwater and non-point sources of pollution. The new protocol committed the governments to cleaning up "areas of concern," which were mostly targeted because of their contaminated sediments. There were also problems with inadequately treated wastewater, non-point source pollution, inland contaminated sites or degraded habitat to a greater degree than the rest of the Great Lakes.

Few of the 43 areas selected have since received a clean bill of health. Twelve were located wholly within Canada, while 26 lay solely within the United States. Five were shared by both countries. Canada has cleaned up and delisted three of its sites, while the U.S. has delisted one. The Conservative government's 2010 budget committed $8 million per year to continue restoration work in affected areas.

In the latest move to update the agreement, the two federal governments asked the IJC in 2005 to check with the public on how well it thinks the agreement is working and what needs improvement. The commission also provided its advice to the governments on these issues, saying a stronger, more contemporary agreement is needed. The commission called for accelerated progress, greater governmental accountability and more public involvement in protecting and restoring the waters of the Great Lakes basin ecosystem. The IJC also wants the agreement to be properly funded so that it can produce significant results more rapidly. That report was handed over in 2006, and formal negotiations to amend the agreement finally began in January 2010.

While progress has been slower than some people would like in the Great Lakes area, more serious head butting has occurred farther west. In BC, a mine proposed in the mid-1980s for the Flathead River basin caused concerns about the welfare of the bull trout, a popular game fish. The river flows into Montana, but the fish were known to spawn beside the proposed coal mine site. The two governments asked the IJC to investigate, and when the commission was done it recommended the mine not be built until the risks were acceptable to both countries and it could be demonstrated that the potential impacts on the sport fishery would either not occur or could be fully mitigated. The mine was not built, though a private sector proposal for a similar project in British Columbia came up again recently. The BC government squashed those plans in its 2010 throne speech when it declared that mining, oil and gas development and coalbed gas extraction will not be permitted in British Columbia's Flathead Valley. The government also said a new partnership with Montana would identify permissible land uses and establish new collaborative approaches to transboundary issues.

IJC Limitations

In Manitoba, concerns about an interbasin transfer project desired by North Dakota has been on the boil since 2000. The Northwest Area Water Supply Project proposes to transfer pre-treated Missouri River water across the continental divide to the city of Minot in the Hudson Bay basin. The Missouri River water would then be treated to drinking water standards and be distributed to a number of communities in the Hudson Bay basin in western North Dakota. The province of Manitoba worries that the minor treatment the Missouri River water will get before it's transferred to the Hudson Bay basin will not be enough to keep invasive species out.

This case draws out the IJC's biggest weakness—a weakness that scares people with concerns about Canada's water sovereignty. The commission's notable limitation is that although it can look into and make *recommendations* on matters that are referred to it by only one of the two parties, it can make *decisions* on matters only if both parties consent to it. In this case, Canada was unable to convince the U.S. to support a joint IJC reference asking for an impartial review of the project.

Other Treaties and Agreements

Some of the other international treaties and agreements reached between Canada and the U.S. include:

• Lake of the Woods Convention and Protocol (1925): This lake overlaps Ontario, Manitoba and Minnesota. The treaty established the desired water level operating range on the lake. A Canadian board regulates the lake on an on-going basis, but its decisions are subject to approval by the International Lake of the Woods Control Board whenever lake levels rise above or fall below certain limits.

• Rainy Lake Convention (1940): This treaty empowers the IJC to determine when emergency conditions exist in the Rainy Lake watershed, which straddles the Ontario–Minnesota border, whether by reason of high or low water. Existing dams can be used to alter water levels.

• Niagara River Water Diversion Treaty (1950): This treaty's purpose is to preserve and enhance the scenic beauty of Niagara Falls and the Niagara River by limiting the amount of water diverted from the Niagara River for power generation.

• Skagit River Treaty (1984): This agreement allowed the city of Seattle to purchase the equivalent amount of hydroelectric power from BC as would have been generated by the raising of the existing Ross Dam. The raising of the dam would have flooded even more of BC, something to which Canadians objected.

Water Sovereignty

Despite the myth of abundance, underneath the surface Canadians must realize the ease with which their water security could evaporate because when it comes to any discussion of exporting water, the majority of us recoil in horror. In the past, polls have pegged disapproval at about 70 percent. But occasionally, the spectre of whether or not we could be *forced* to export water rises up like some sea monster from the depths.

Free Trade

Critics point to our membership in the North American Free Trade Agreement (NAFTA) and the World Trade Organization (WTO) as legal vortices that could suck us into an unwilling deal. "Like the Conservatives before them, the Liberal government declined to negotiate an exemption for freshwater in the text of [NAFTA], even though exemptions had already been negotiated for raw logs and unprocessed fish," wrote Frank Quinn, a water policy expert, in a 2007 paper on water exports and diversions. "Instead, the Prime Minister's Office issued a media release stating that the three governments were in agreement that nothing in NAFTA would oblige the water belonging to any of the parties in its natural state to be exported (Canada, 1993)....How such a statement would be treated in a trade panel hearing is open to question."

The government has repeatedly denied any vulnerability. Environment Canada maintains that position today. "Canada's water belongs to Canadians," the department says. "We are free to manage our water and protect our environment in our own best interests. Nothing in NAFTA or in any of Canada's international trade agreements prevents us from protecting our water. These agreements do not create new obligations for us to sell our water, nor do they limit our ability to adopt laws for managing our own water resources."

To ensure our sovereignty of this precious resource, Canada issued a joint statement with the United States and Mexico in 1993 declaring that NAFTA creates no rights to the natural water resources of any of the countries. Under these trade agreements, water in its natural state—in a lake or a river, for example—is not a tradable good or product (i.e., exportable commodity) and is therefore not subject to the provisions of these agreements, Environment Canada says.

The Slippery Slope of Water Exports

Meanwhile, some of the provinces were experimenting with water exports. Quinn writes that in 1986, BC quietly decided that it would permit entrepreneurs to export small volumes of freshwater from its coastal streams by marine tanker. One of its six licensees, Snowcap, eventually partnered with American firm Sun Belt, which wanted to ship the water to a drought-stricken California community. But a flood of new export applications, following the news of the Snowcap agreement, triggered a public uproar. The province put a moratorium on new or expanded licences. That meant Snowcap couldn't get enough additional water to fulfill its contract. Although the province reimbursed Snowcap for its out-of-pocket expenses, it refused to recognize Sun Belt, which was not named on the licence. Sun Belt's American owner threatened to sue Canada under Article 11 of NAFTA but has since apparently given up his action, Quinn writes.

Entrepreneurs were also scouting coastal regions in the Atlantic Provinces and Quebec for possible water sources, Quinn adds. In 1996, the Newfoundland government agreed to allow export of freshwater in bulk by ship, subject to conditions of environmental assessment and benefits to the provincial economy. The Quebec government was engaged in reviewing water export opportunities and their competitive position vis-à-vis world markets.

But it was the Nova Group case that really spooked everyone into action. The Sault Ste. Marie newspaper broke the news in April 1998. A local company named Nova Group was granted permission to take up to 600 million litres of water annually from Lake Superior and send it to Asian markets via ocean tanker.

Lake Superior is a vast body of water—it's said that the lake could contain all the other Great Lakes, plus three more Lake Eries. So the volume of water wanted by Nova Group wasn't the issue. A big part of the problem was the ease with which the company had obtained its permit—and for a mere $50, according to the Council of Canadians.

It was a regional office of the Ontario Ministry of the Environment that gave the company its permit. "No other government on either side of the international boundary had been consulted about the proposal, even the Ministry's sister water agency, the Ministry of Natural Resources," Quinn wrote about the incident. "The volume of water to be removed was an insignificant fraction of the lake, and the economics of the venture were dubious. The problem was the setting of precedent: governments at all levels in Canada and the United States were concerned about other entrepreneurs following suit and the much larger cumulative effect of such initiatives on the Great Lakes–St. Lawrence River system."

The fear of withdrawals decimating such large lakes is not unfounded. One need only look at the example of the Aral Sea in Kazakhstan and Uzbekistan. Once the fourth largest lake in the world, it took only a few decades of intense irrigation to destroy it. The lake now exists as pitiful fragments of its former self.

Quinn says Ontario was embarrassed by Nova Group's easy access to water and took steps to rescind the permit. Soon after, in 1999, Ontario prohibited water transfers out of the province's three major water basins. Quebec also moved that year, enforcing a temporary moratorium on the export of water. The Water Resources Preservation Act prohibited the transfer of water outside of Quebec but had a few exceptions, including water taken to produce electric power and water packaged for human consumption in containers of 20 litres capacity or less. The moratorium became permanent in 2001.

Satellite Photos of the Aral Sea in 1989 and 2008

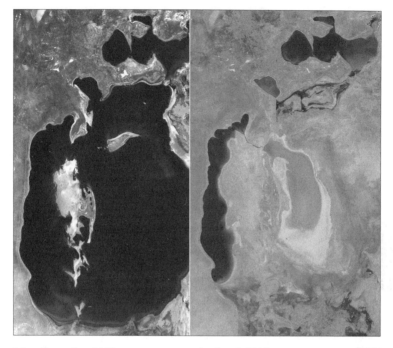

July – September, 1989   *October 5, 2008*

Meanwhile, Ottawa and Washington had jointly asked the International Joint Commission to investigate the implications of consumption, diversion and export on Great Lakes waters. In 2000, the commission delivered its report, recommending that the governments of the Great Lakes states and Ontario and Quebec should not permit water to be removed from the Great Lakes basin unless, at a minimum, the proponent can demonstrate that the removal would not endanger the integrity of the Great Lakes basin ecosystem. "If all interests in the Basin are considered," the commission explained, "there is never a 'surplus' of water in the Great Lakes system; every drop of water has several potential uses, and trade-offs must be made when, through human intervention, waters are removed from the system." This lack of surplus is underscored by the fact that less than one percent of Great Lakes waters are renewed annually through precipitation and runoff.

Expanding on their primary recommendation, the IJC suggested water removal should only be allowed if:

- there are no practical alternatives for obtaining the water

- full consideration is given to the potential cumulative impacts of the proposed removal, taking into account the possibility of similar proposals in the foreseeable future

- effective conservation practices will be implemented in the place to which the water would be sent

- sound planning practices will be applied with respect to the proposed removal, and, there is no net loss to the area from which the water is taken and, in any event, there is no greater than a five percent loss (the average loss of all consumptive uses within the Great Lakes basin)

- the water will be returned in a condition that, using the best available technology, protects the quality of, and prevents the introduction of alien invasive species into, the waters of the Great Lakes.

In Canada, the federal government felt pressure to do something decisive and more encompassing about the threat of water exports. But trade lawyers and policy experts advised Environment Canada that they could not adapt the Canada Water Preservation Act to prohibit water export from Canada, Quinn says. The reason? "Neither NAFTA nor the World Trade Organization would tolerate a country restricting water explicitly for use within national boundaries," he writes. "This would be trade discrimination."

Quinn continues, "So to provide a workable interpretation of constitutional as well as trade law, the federal government proposed a cooperative approach, in which the provinces (and territories) would enact or amend their laws or regulations to prohibit bulk water removal from watersheds within their jurisdictions, and the federal government would enact amendments to its International

Boundary Waters Treaty Act to accomplish the same purpose within the Canadian portion of boundary waters. This strategy was announced by the Government of Canada, and all senior governments except for New Brunswick (not an obvious target for water export) have since addressed the issue in one way or another, albeit reluctantly on the part of some provinces."

In December 2002, an act amending the treaty came into force, prohibiting anyone from removing more than 50,000 litres of water a day from boundary waters. So we do have more protection on the Great Lakes now than we did before, Quinn, now retired, says during an interview. "And we could stop another similar proposal like Nova Group put forward. They couldn't do that today.

"On the other hand, if somebody had approval to take water from the Fraser River, that's not a boundary water, then we would depend on British Columbia to do something about that," he adds. "The trouble with that is each province has gone about it a different way. And we're not sure that what each of the provinces has done would pass muster in terms of NAFTA or the World Trade Organization or whether it would look like it's just aimed at stopping trade. The bad part about each province going and doing it by themselves is some of them did it in a pretty loose fashion and may not stand up to international scrutiny. But also, provinces like Quebec and Newfoundland in particular are saying, 'Well, there's not much chance in making money on exporting water by ship today, but we might be interested in doing that in 10 years.' So there's always that possibility that where each party looks after itself, we don't have any national control over this at all."

Under this scenario, Quinn says each province must tread carefully, especially because there are still uncertainties about obligations under NAFTA and the WTO agreement. "Obviously if you get involved in international trade in water, if the province allows the shipments to go and it develops, but then changes its mind two years later, well it might be pretty hard to pull back. Still, it would just be that province that would be caught in it. If Newfoundland sends a few shiploads somewhere, it doesn't mean any party can take water from elsewhere in Canada. Though there are some environmental groups who would argue that."

Quinn says you can't get involved in the water trade and then turn the tap off, especially when dealing with the United States. If they lavish billions on infrastructure for diversion, he says, then we can't expect to be able to change our minds five years later if we're not really happy with the agreement.

Protecting the Great Lakes

In the Great Lakes basin, there was a more focused effort to get all the jurisdictions to protect the lakes in a consistent, cohesive manner. The eight states and two provinces had already taken steps toward this: in 1985 they signed a Great Lakes Charter, which aimed to protect and conserve the waters of the basin; and in 2001 the same parties signed a supplementary agreement to the charter known as the Great Lakes Charter Annex. Following the Nova Group scare, they committed to creating something more binding within the next three years.

This commitment turned into a lengthy struggle to formalize efforts to stop water from leaving the basin. Negotiations were particularly protracted and often heated in the U.S. because the eight basin states have a wide spectrum of attitudes toward the lakes. Journalist Peter Annin, who is widely considered a leading authority on Great Lakes water issues, says each jurisdiction has its own "water personality."

"Michigan is adamantly opposed to diversions, but balks at limitations on its own in-Basin consumptive use," he wrote in his book *The Great Lakes Water Wars.* "New York has major hydropower considerations. Illinois is worried about maintaining its U.S. Supreme Court–mandated water allocation that keeps metropolitan Chicago alive. Ontario shares many of Michigan's anti-diversion sentiments, and Quebec, at the tail end of the system, is concerned about what everyone else does upstream. Minnesota has been the most progressive water jurisdiction in the Basin—Indiana decidedly less so—with Wisconsin, Ohio and Pennsylvania somewhere in between."

Whatever their differences, the 10 members knew they had to work together to protect their common resource. The states were given legal advice that they couldn't sign an international water treaty with the provinces, Annin wrote, but the provinces could adopt similar statutes on their side of the border, thereby surrounding the lakes with a parallel water-management structure.

The parties soon figured out that it would take two separate documents, not one, to forge the protection they needed. The one that involved Canada was the Great Lakes–St. Lawrence River Basin Sustainable Water Resources Agreement. Signed in December 2005, this "good-faith" agreement between the two provinces and eight states pledged that they would "act together to protect, conserve and restore the Waters of the Great Lakes–St. Lawrence River Basin..." Although Ontario Premier Dalton McGuinty attended the signing, only two state governors were there, and Quebec did not send its premier. The National Assembly of Quebec approved the agreement almost a year later in November 2006.

On the American side of the border, the Great Lakes–St. Lawrence River Basin Water Resources Compact was a binding agreement between the eight states to do the same. But as Annin pointed out, the compact wouldn't become law until it was pushed through all eight of their legislatures and the U.S. Congress. It was a long wait. The state legislatures ratified the agreements, one by one, during 2007 and 2008. Then the U.S. Senate and House of Representatives approved the legislation in August and September 2008 respectively. Finally, President George Bush signed it into law in October 2008.

Meanwhile, both Ontario and Quebec forged ahead to make good on the agreement they had signed, as it came with certain implementation expectations. Ontario claimed that it was "already a leader in water protection, having passed strict rules banning water diversions out of the province's three major water basins—the Great Lakes-St. Lawrence River Basin, the Hudson Bay Basin and the Nelson River Basin." As a result, "Ontario's laws already met or exceeded many of the requirements of the Great Lakes agreement. In negotiating the agreement, Ontario sought similar protection by all Great Lakes jurisdictions," the government said.

By mid-2007, Ontario had introduced the Safeguarding and Sustaining Ontario's Water Act. It elevated Ontario's existing ban on interbasin transfers from regulation to legislation. It also banned new or increased transfers of water from one Great Lake watershed to another (i.e., intra-basin transfers) and allowed the other nine Great Lake jurisdictions judicial review of Ontario water withdrawal and transfer decisions.

But there are still water activists who believe Ontario has failed to deal with key concerns. For one thing, it allows water in containers under 20 litres to be exempt from prohibitions on diversion, says an open letter from Inside the Bottle, a Polaris Institute campaign against bottled water. "This includes most of the bottled water that is being extracted from the Great Lakes Basin in Ontario by Coca-Cola, Pepsi, Nestlé, and Aquafarms 93 (which bottles for other retail outlets including Wal-Mart, Shoppers Drug Mart, and Loblaws)," says the letter. The bottled water industry is growing and transports its product outside of Ontario and Canada, the activists point out. Another worry is that the act gives the ultimate decision-making power on bulk water diversions to a tribunal, with no assurance that the people of Ontario or the public interest are adequately represented.

Grand Diversion Schemes of the Past
...and Maybe the Future?

While there have been a few large diversion projects built in Canada, few were as ambitious as two schemes brought forward in the late 1950s and early 1960s by engineers. The North American Water and Power Alliance (NAWAPA) project was proposed by a southern California engineering firm called Ralph M. Parsons and Co. The plan was to divert water from Alaska, Yukon and BC and send it south via a massive reservoir and canal river system.

The plan involved yoking the Rocky Mountain trench as a multitasking storage vessel and canal. The trench is a valley that stretches 1400 kilometres from northern BC down to Montana. From the trench, some of the water would head east through the Peace River in Alberta and all the way out to Lake Superior through a combination of canals and existing rivers. The rest of the water would be directed south through Montana and Idaho to Nevada, California, Arizona and northern Mexico. A massive amount of hydropower would be generated as the water journeyed east and south. The project would be bolstered on its eastern end with spurs heading down from James Bay and northeastern Quebec.

In his classic book *Cadillac Desert*, Marc Reisner wrote, "In the 1960s, when anything big and brutish got at least a passing nod of attention, the NAWAPA scheme excited a considerable spasm of interest." Some exploratory discussions were apparently held between Canada and the U.S. Secretary of State at the time, Reisner writes. "In the 1970s, however, as the environmental movement and Canadian nation waxed, NAWAPA's fortunes waned."

The cost of the project in 1963 was estimated at $100 billion, and the engineers thought it would take 20 years to construct. "The proponents suggested that 33 U.S. states, seven provinces or territories in Canada and three northern states in Mexico would benefit directly," wrote the International Joint Commission in a 1985 report on diversions and consumptive uses. While the commission allowed that the "total list of benefits is extensive," it said that no additional work has been done since the project was first conceived to address issues such as the technical feasibility, the enormous economic costs and the social and ecological effects.

Reisner said it would be Canada that would have to suffer the worst of the environmental consequences, "and they would be phenomenal…Every significant river between Anchorage and Vancouver would have to be dammed for power or water, or both—the Tanana, the Yukon, the Copper, the Taku, the Skeena, the Stikine, the Liard, the Bella Coola, the Dean, the Chilcotin and the Fraser. All of these have prolific salmon fisheries, which would be largely, if not wholly, destroyed."

It's not shocking, then, that Canadians have mostly given the project a firm "pass," but NAWAPA still bobs up now and again. Most recently, the editor of a small paper in Virginia announced in 2009 that he was going to make it his mission to promote the project. Nicholas Benton says he helped promote the project back in the 1980s with former Utah Senator Frank Moss. He thinks the project's time has come, as it would create tens of thousands of jobs during a time when the U.S. has a high unemployment rate.

The eastern version of NAWAPA—the GRAND project—is still being promoted by its creator, Thomas Kierans. Now 97 years old and living in Newfoundland, Kierans worries we won't be able to meet the water needs of North America's growing population. "Before the end of the century we will have a billion people living on the continent," he says in an interview. "It's the major job that Canada has got to solve."

He's been thinking about water needs for decades now, beginning in 1933 at the age of 20. It was in the midst of the Dust Bowl years, and he was passing through Saskatoon at the time. He remembers standing at the railway station and being barely able to make out the construction site of the Bessborough Hotel. "I could only see a block because of the dust."

That's when he decided he'd do something to bring water to the parched prairies—and beyond. He called his idea the Great Recycling and Northern Development Canal of North America, or GRAND Canal. His idea was to capture the freshwater flowing into James Bay using a series of outflow-only, sea-level dikes constructed across the northern end of James Bay. The dikes would capture the freshwater just before it mixes with the saltwater of Hudson Bay.

The point of capture of this water is key to Kierans. "I'm against diversions," he says. "That is being really un-Canadian when you propose to divert water. My proposal is to recycle water after it has finished its job on land. Its flow should not be interrupted until it reaches sea level."

Once the outflow of as many as 11 rivers is captured in the newly formed lake, it would be pumped into the Harricana River, crossing into the Great Lakes watershed near Amos, Quebec, into Lake Timiskaming and the Ottawa River, crossing near Mattawa, Ontario, into Lake Nipissing and the French River to Lake Huron. Kierans allows that there would be changes along the route, including enlargement of the French River. But once the water reached Lake Huron, it would free up the water that normally runs from Lake Superior into Lake Huron, and water could be pumped west out of Lake Superior, Kierans reasoned. From there, water would be directed to the Canadian prairies to water money-making crops. Then it would head south into the U.S., branching out to quench the thirst of almost the entire Southwest. Kierans said the project would also offer flood control.

He acknowledges the project would be costly—somewhere from $100 billion to as much as $300 billion—but "we're not talking small problems," he says. "Nothing's free." And money would be made as well. People pay to get water now, and this project wouldn't change that, he says.

Not everyone was convinced, though. "While some assert that the project would have multiple economic and other benefits," the IJC opined, "others argue that the direct costs are astronomical and that the project is likely to have devastating and irreversible ecological effects, particularly for inhabitants of northern Canada."

The impacts are predicted to include detrimental effects to fish and marine mammals in Hudson Bay, according to Robert Milko, who wrote a paper on the topic that was published in the journal *Arctic* in 1986. That's because the dike would divert 61 percent of Hudson Bay's freshwater south, also changing the cycle of ice formation and melt. Changes to coastal staging areas in both Hudson Bay and James Bay would most likely destroy a major portion of the North American migratory bird population, Milko wrote.

The project did have fans, though, including the rather high-profile Robert Bourassa, premier of Quebec. Bourassa held a strong belief in hydroelectric power, which he backed in the early 1970s by starting the James Bay hydroelectric project. Kierans helped write chapter nine in Bourassa's book *Power from the North*, which talks about the GRAND Canal.

There have been other studies looking at ways to move water from places of plenitude to scarcity. One looked at moving water from Lake Superior into the Missouri River basin to make up for water diverted to the Ogallala region. The cost of the 18 pumping plants, seven 1000-megawatt power plants and 984 kilometres of conveyance was estimated at about $27 billion, says the IJC.

Ultimately, these projects were stopped by a combination of factors—exorbitant cost, resistance from local people, fear of environmental impacts. The question will always remain, though: could a crack in the dam of this opposition ever allow a project like these ones to proceed?

PART THREE

The Future of Water

Will there be enough water
When my ship comes in?
—The Dead Weather

Each generation judges those that came before from its unique station in time. Remember those stories about the old settlers and buffalo hunters shooting bison from train windows just for fun? Who today would not shake their heads at that story? What a waste. The practice helped push the population off a cliff, plunging from as high as 70 million animals to near extinction. The passenger pigeon, a bird that once roamed in flocks so large they darkened the sky, suffered similar exploitation, plus the destruction of its food supply, and is now extinct. It boggles the modern mind.

But what will future generations say about us? What will make them raise their eyebrows, tsk-tsk disapprovingly or get downright angry about our wanton carelessness? I'm sure there are countless transgressions that would fit the bill, but surely some would centre around our use—or misuse—of water.

CHAPTER SEVEN

Changing Attitudes

PERHAPS FUTURE GENERATIONS will take issue with the fact that some of us washed our driveways with water. That we let the tap run when we brushed our teeth. That we pumped freshwater down into congested oil wells in order to push out a bit more black gold, knowingly taking that water out of the hydrological cycle. Perhaps that we used water to grow potatoes in the near-desert of southern Alberta.

There are plenty of people who already consider these behaviours sinful. But that doesn't include the majority; otherwise, surely there would be laws against such waste. In fact, a 2010 survey shows that plenty of us engage in wasteful water ways of life. The survey said that 19 percent of respondents hose down their driveways, while surely each of those people owns a broom. Almost half of those surveyed leave the water running while brushing their teeth (46 percent) or rinsing the dishes (44 percent). Some of these people are also part of the group of 78 percent who believe they try hard to conserve freshwater in the course of their daily activities and the 83 percent who say they are concerned about the declining state of the availability of Canada's freshwater.

Many of those surveyed in this Ipsos Reid poll also admitted to engaging in water-contaminating activities, including allowing soapy water to run down a storm drain (i.e. when washing a car) (21 percent) and using soap or shampoo to bathe in a lake (16 percent). And yet one-half (49 percent) believe freshwater is

Canada's most important natural resource—more than forests (20 percent), agriculture (17 percent), oil (9 percent), fisheries (3 percent), metals (1 percent) or coal (0 percent).

"There is an obvious disconnect between Canadians' attitudes toward water conservation and what they're actually doing," said Bob Sandford, chairman of the Canadian Partnership Initiative of the UN Water for Life Decade, when the numbers were released. "Canadians say they are much more concerned about the availability and quantity of fresh water than any other natural resource, yet their efforts to conserve water are actually decreasing. This should be a huge concern, given that we live in a society run by water and the long-term supply of this precious resource is already at risk in many parts of the country."

How Much Do We Use?

Canadians have a reputation for using almost more water per person than any other nationality. The most recent publicly available data shows that in 2006, water use in Canada amounted to 60,527 million cubic metres. That's 60.5 trillion litres. About one-third of this water is consumed, while the rest was returned to the waterbodies from which it was taken, Environment Canada says.

So what do we lavish all this water upon? It seems we don't have a firm grip on this—another symptom of thinking we have more than enough. But Environment Canada cobbled together data it collected from municipalities in 2006 with Statistics Canada information on industrial (2005) and agricultural (2001) use to come up with the following rough estimates. A full 63 percent was used to generate thermal power, such as that created when coal or natural gas is burned. The manufacturing sector required 15 percent. Municipal use rang in at 9.5 percent. Agriculture also used 9.5 percent, and mining used 1 percent. They did not account for the missing two percent.

Major Water Use in Canada
(Industrial, Municipal and Agricultural)

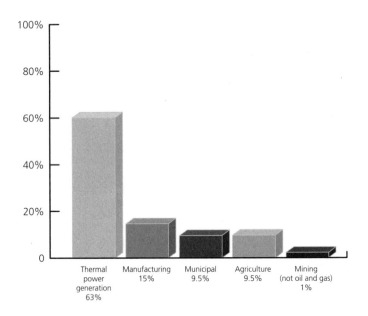

A closer look at power production reveals that 140 litres of water are required to produce one kilowatt hour (kWh) of electricity in a fossil fuel plant. A nuclear power plant requires even more water: 205 litres per kWh. Some of this water is converted to steam to drive the generator producing the electricity, Environment Canada explains. "Most of the water, however, is used for condenser cooling. Why is so much cooling necessary? Because today's processes can only convert 40 percent of the fuel's energy into usable electricity. The rest is wasted. This shows the double costs of inefficient energy use: first, in the waste energy, and then in the water required to cool the wasted heat to the temperature where it can be released safely into the environment. This requires a continuous flow of cooling water circulating through the condenser."

Canada's Water Footprint

Everything has a water footprint—a concept that gained ground in recent years following in the steps of the better known "ecological footprint" introduced in the 1990s by Canadian William Rees. The water footprint concept, created by Dutch water management professor Arjen Hoekstra, can be calculated for an individual, community, business and country. For a nation, it's defined as the volume of water needed for the production of the goods and services consumed by the inhabitants of the country. In 2007, Hoekstra and Ashok Chapagain published research on the water footprints of nations. They also quantified how much water was needed to produce crops such as wheat in different countries, and how much water it took to make a cotton T-shirt or a microchip.

How many litres of water does it take to produce:

1 glass of beer: 75

1 apple: 70

1 cotton T-shirt: 2000

1 hamburger: 2400

1 pair of bovine leather shoes: 8000

1 microchip: 32

1 tomato: 13

1 automobile: 120,000

The tricky part of calculating a country's water footprint is thinking about everything the people in that country consume, regardless of whether or not it's produced domestically. "A water expert being asked to assess the water demand in a particular country will generally add the water withdrawals for the different sectors of the economy," Hoekstra and Chapagain wrote. "Although useful information, this does not tell much about the water actually needed by the people in the country in relation to their consumption pattern. The fact is that many goods consumed by the inhabitants of a country are produced in other countries, which means that it can happen that the real water demand of a population is much higher than the national water withdrawals do suggest. The reverse can be the case as well: national water withdrawals are substantial, but a large amount of the products are being exported for consumption elsewhere." The idea of the water footprint is tied to the concept of virtual water, meaning the amount of water polluted or consumed while producing food or other products.

Water scarce countries can buy water-intensive products from other countries, leaving themselves more water.

Canada does not have a flattering water footprint—there's no light ballet-slipper tip-toeing going on here. It's more likely a steel-toed boot tromp and kick. While the average of the 21 countries chosen in the study is 1240 cubic metres per capita per year, Canada's is 2049. Only Italy, Thailand and the U.S. had higher rates. The authors say there are four important direct factors explaining high water footprints:

1. The total volume of consumption, which is generally related to gross national income of a country.

2. Individuals have a water-intensive consumption pattern. For example, high consumption of meat significantly contributes to a high water footprint. This factor partially explains the high water footprint of countries such as the U.S., Canada, France, Spain, Portugal, Italy and Greece. Next to meat consumption,

high consumption of industrial goods significantly contributes to the total water footprints of rich countries.

3. Climate. In regions with a high evaporative demand, the water requirement per unit of crop production is relatively large. This factor partially explains the high water footprint in countries such as Senegal, Mali, Sudan, Chad, Nigeria and Syria.

4. Water-inefficient agricultural practice, which means that water productivity in terms of output per drop of water is relatively low. This factor partly explains the high water footprint of countries such as Thailand, Cambodia, Turkmenistan, Sudan, Mali and Nigeria.

Hoekstra and Chapagain say there are many ways to reduce footprints. "A first way is to break the seemingly obvious link between economic growth and increased water use, for instance by adopting production techniques that require less water per unit of product. Water productivity in agriculture can be improved for instance by applying advanced techniques of rainwater harvesting and supplementary irrigation. A second way of reducing water footprints is to shift to consumption patterns that require less water, for instance by reducing meat consumption."

The authors doubt cutting meat consumption is a feasible road, as the world-wide trend shows meat consumption tends to increase rather than decrease. They suspect a broader and subtler approach involving pricing, raising awareness, product labelling and other incentives will be needed. The general public, though often aware of energy requirements, knows little about the water needed to produce goods and services, they say. In Canada this lack of understanding is reflected somewhat by the 2010 poll that shows that even at home, three in ten (29 percent) say they don't know what they pay for their water each month, three times the proportion (10 percent) who are in the dark about their electricity bill.

Hoekstra and Chapagain say there is a third method to reduce water footprints: shift production from areas with low water productivity to areas with high water productivity, thus increasing global water use efficiency. They give the example of Jordan successfully externalizing its water footprint by importing wheat and rice products from the U.S., which has higher water productivity than Jordan. When 75 percent of a country has a desert climate, it is obviously unwise to attempt full-blown wheat and rice growing. But would countries sacrifice production of a cash crop or manufactured good if they had enough water to manage, but another country could produce the same item using less water?

A Closer Look at Canada's Water Use

It's difficult to get a firm grasp on exactly how much water we use. Frank Quinn, a former water policy adviser with Environment Canada, says the department had a person leading the collection of water use information in the 1990s, but that person retired and it's not being done anymore. "Nobody knows really how much water we're using in Canada. We can get a rough estimate and that's about it. It's really disgraceful." The lack of consistent data means the department can't show what's happening over a period of time, he says.

There is some spotty data trickling in, with the latest data from 2005 showing that Canadians, on average, used 320 litres of water per person per day. Over one-third of that (35 percent) went to showers and baths, about another third (30 percent) to toilets. Laundry used up one-fifth (20 percent), one-tenth (10 percent) was used in the kitchen and for drinking. And cleaning accounted for the last one-twentieth (5 percent). A more recent, but limited, survey of households supplied by 34 water utilities across Canada, found that the median volume of water used was 243 litres per day in 2007.

How Water is Consumed in the Home

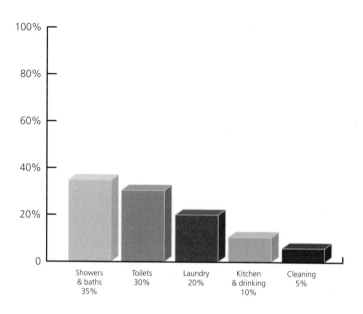

Humans definitely need water for survival—it makes up about 60 percent of our body weight. But it takes only a few litres of water each day to replace the liquid we lose through breathing, sweating and defecating. A healthy, sedentary male in a climate like ours needs about 3.7 litres of water each day, according to the American Institute of Medicine of the National Academies. That amount includes intake from all beverages and foods. The average woman needs 2.7 litres per day. So obviously we're able to get far more water than is necessary to meet our survival needs.

Peter Gleick, an internationally recognized water expert, expanded the concept of basic water requirements in a 1996 paper in which he said people also need water for hygiene, sanitation services and modest household needs like food preparation. He calculated this would add up to 50 liters per person per day. Doing the math, this means Canadians were using 279 litres over and above basic needs each day in 2004.

The rest of the developed world sometimes looks askance at our profligate water habits. Canada has been criticized repeatedly by the Organization for Economic Cooperation and Development (OECD) for our excessive use of water, notes David Boyd in a 2001 report that compares our performance to other countries in the organization. "Since 1980, overall water use in Canada has increased by 25.7 percent. This is five times higher than the overall OECD increase of 4.5 percent. In contrast, nine OECD nations were able to decrease their overall water use since 1980."

Water use continues to rise despite an increase in cost to consumers. Since 1991, the national average price for residential municipal water and wastewater service for a monthly consumption of 25 cubic metres—what an average family uses—has increased from $25.88 in 1991 to $40.47 in 2004. That's a 56 percent increase. But Environment Canada insists that although prices have increased steadily, in general water prices in Canada continue to remain low compared to the actual cost of providing these services. "Canadian water prices have traditionally been among the lowest in the Organization for Economic Cooperation and Development," the department says. Compared to the other member countries, Canada had the second lowest price for household water, with only Hungary charging less per cubic metre. Households in the Netherlands, France and the United Kingdom paid up to four times what Canadians were charged. Industrial water prices, however, were fairly similar across the 12 countries.

As anyone could logically deduce, there's a solid relationship between conserving water and charging more for it. Amount of water consumption is also related to charging for water on a flat rate or metered basis. This relationship is borne out in an Environment Canada report on 2004 data that shows that flat rates resulted in daily water use of 467 litres per person, while people under metered or volume-based rates used 266 litres each day.

The difference has been consistent: consumption is always 70 to 80 percent higher under flat rates, Environment Canada says.

Canada retains an astonishing number of unmetered households, though the percentage of residential clients that are metered did rise from 52 percent in 1991 to 63 percent in 2004. There's a clear difference between smaller municipalities and larger ones. In 2004, 64 percent of residents in municipalities with 2000 to 5000 residents were on flat rates, while only 24 percent of residents in cities with populations over 500,000 were billed this way.

There is some conflicting information coming out of the Great Lakes basin, though. "Public water systems currently account for the bulk of consumptive use, comprising one-third of the total, and withdrawals in this category have been increasing in recent years despite the decline in total withdrawals," says the State of the Great Lakes 2009 report. "Higher water prices have been widely advocated in order to reduce water demand. Observers have noted that European per capita water use is only half the North American level, while prices in Europe are twice as high. However, economists have found that both residential and industrial water demand in the United States and Canada are relatively insensitive to price changes. The over-consumption of water in North America may be more a product of lifestyle and lax attitudes."

Higher prices may still be crucial for providing public water systems with capital for repairs, the report adds, as this can prevent water losses by fixing system leaks, for example. "But reducing the underlying demand may require other strategies in addition to price increases, such as public education on resource conservation and promotion of water-saving technologies."

What Can Be Done?

Water-saving Fixtures

There are a couple of easy targets in every home. Toilets and showers swallow a huge share of every home's water budget. Unflappable homeowners, not cowed by a bit of plumbing, are installing water-saving fixtures. Between 1994 and 2007, the percentage of households with a low-flow shower head rose from 44 percent to 62 percent, Statistics Canada says. The use of reduced-volume toilets increased substantially as well, more than doubling from 15 percent in 1994 to 39 percent in 2007. In its previous report, the agency had a theory about the rapid adoption: "Water and energy prices rose quicker than average between 1994 and 2006. Increasing relative costs may have provided a financial signal for households to retrofit to water-saving fixtures."

Of course, that financial signal is missed by many people who rent. "Renters do not always have control over the type of water fixtures used in their dwelling, nor are they usually responsible for water bills, so there is less motivation for these households to spend the money or time to retrofit," Statistics Canada noted. Those differences show up when the numbers are broken down: low-flow shower heads were installed by 63 percent of owned homes and 45 percent of rented homes, while reduced-volume toilets were in 43 percent of owned homes and 23 percent of rented homes.

People with more money were also more likely to install water-saving fixtures. In 2006, households with annual incomes below $25,000 were less likely to use both low-flow showers (52 percent) and reduced-volume toilets (33 percent) than households that had annual incomes in excess of $75,000. Targeted grants or subsidies could help these lower income households make the switch, a task they would be more likely to tackle if they were also educated about the potential cost-saving benefit.

No province in Canada prohibits the sale and installation of 13- and 20-litre toilet models, according to a 2007 report by the Canadian Mortgage and Housing Corporation (CMHC). "As such, Canada is behind most of the developed countries of the world, including the U.S., when it comes to reducing toilet water consumption." The use of 6-litre toilets is mandated across the entire United States and is considered standard in most parts of Europe, the corporation says.

Canadian authorities are getting pressure to legislate against these water pigs, though. The Canadian Water and Wastewater Association has been campaigning for this legislation for years. The association even spearheaded, and now posts, a performance report on 6-litre toilets, which are put through their paces with a cylinder of soybean paste "having similar properties to human waste."

The CMHC says the hesitancy to prohibit the 13- and 20-litre toilets appears to stem from two concerns: the perception that efficient toilets do not perform well, and the perception that efficient toilets do not provide enough water to adequately transport waste to the sewer. The first concern was addressed through the afore-mentioned toilet testing program, which the CMHC also supports. To date, the program has identified more than 200 models that are almost certain to exceed customer expectations for performance. The second concern regarding the ability of water-efficient toilets to transport waste to the sewer was dealt with by a CMHC study, which proved there was no issue.

In all of this adoption, Ontario appeared to be leading the way due, at least in part, to regulatory changes to the Ontario Building Code in 1996, which made the use of water-saving fixtures mandatory for all new structures. In the spring of 2010, Ontario announced a proposal to require that all toilets sold in the province use no more than six litres of water per flush. BC also requires low-flow toilets In all new construction and renovation but seems to be the only other province to have done so thus far. Many other municipalities across the country have taken the initiative though, enacting bylaws requiring low-flow toilets.

Government Regulation

Regulation is a key part of changing water use rates. Governments have a critical role to play in changing water use habits. If Canadians receive good governance from all levels of government, there should be no obstacles to achieving efficient, appropriate water use. This means regulation of all kinds, on prices, devices, allocation and reuse, say Karen Bakker and Kathryn Furlong in a 2008 policy report. The duo focused their research on the relationship between governance and sustainable water management practices by municipal water supply utilities. They talked to experts and people working in municipalities to figure out what had to change. "A key issue in advancing water conservation is a lack of accountability for sustainable water use at all levels of government," they wrote. "The problem of insufficient accountability is often identified as a lack of political will."

And that political will can't be a flash in the pan, either. "Analysts at the Policy Research Initiative argue that it is an absence of sustained leadership and political will and not the nature of the governance strategy itself that limits progress on sustainable development in Canada," Bakker and Furlong wrote. "They find Canada's federal sustainable development governance strategy to be as functionally sound as that of European countries whose approaches have produced tangible and impressive results (e.g., Germany, The Netherlands and Denmark)." Once everyone agrees on a vision for water management, it's necessary to bolster that vision with quantitative long-term targets, interim milestones and ongoing monitoring and reporting, the analysts added in their 2002 report.

If governments are tackling the water conservation issue, it appears to be a pretty low key affair. The 2010 Ipsos Reid survey showed only one in three people were aware of local government initiatives to conserve water. Awareness is highest in British Columbia (47 percent), Saskatchewan and Manitoba, (38 percent), Ontario (35 percent) and Alberta (32 percent) and lower in Atlantic Canada (22 percent) and Quebec (21 percent).

One of the best approaches for dealing with water challenges is called integrated water resource management, the federal policy agency says in a 2009 report. This flexible, place-based approach brings together the authorities responsible for making water management decisions with all the interests that depend on that water. "The resulting arrangement will be unique in each case as participation will depend on the level of water use, the types of water use, the types of challenges the area is facing, and the geographic scale at which these uses and challenges interact." Currently, there are at least 115 decentralized governance arrangements at the provincial or territorial level in Canada that play important roles in making water management governance structures more integrated and place-based, the report says.

Although it is widely acknowledged that this watershed-based, tailor-made approach is best suited to dealing with water issues, its specialist nature also makes it vulnerable. In each watershed there are key sectors that need to get along, and in each watershed these sectors will be represented by different people— whose personalities may clash. The size of the watershed in question can vary each time, as can the nature of the problem that is bringing together people in the first place. And each time there may be a different mix of authorities—federal, provincial, municipal—needed at the table. Again, this depends on the problem.

The bottom line is that there are no cookie-cutter solutions to be handed over to each watershed. But there are things the federal government can do to make things easier, the analysts say. One of the strongest contributions will be providing standardized data and science of the water resources in question. Figuring out what the in-stream flow need is and then managing water use to meet that need will be a key goal for each of the watershed organizations. "It is clear that as pressures on the availability of water resources build, the federal government will be obliged to make difficult and potentially contentious decisions to fulfill its responsibilities and ensure that in-stream flow needs are met in situations of decreasing availability and increasing demand," the analysts wrote.

A crucial piece of ecological information is called the in-stream flow need. This term refers to the amount of water over time that is necessary to protect aquatic eco-systems. For example, a certain species of fish could require specific water levels during a particular season in order to spawn successfully.

What Each Canadian Can Do

There are some very simple things individual Canadians can do to reduce water use and protect water supplies from contamination:

• As mentioned earlier, install low-flow toilets and shower heads. Never flush garbage or expired medication down the toilet.

• Always repair leaky faucets.

• Don't run water continuously while brushing your teeth. Same goes for kitchen activities such as washing dishes or vegetables and fruits. Partially fill the sink and use that water instead. A quick rinse afterward will finish the job. And storing a pitcher of water in the fridge means you don't need to run the tap to get a cool drink.

• Always fill the washing machine and dishwasher to capacity. Use detergents that are biodegradable and don't contain phosphates.

• Water indoor plants with water from a rain barrel.

• Water lawns and gardens on cool, windless mornings. Using water from rain barrels is ideal, but if you're using a sprinkler make sure it isn't overshooting onto pavement. Better yet, select a drip or trickle irrigation system to deliver water efficiently to the roots of plants that need it. If a sprinkler is used, select one with a timer that sprays the water close to the ground. Lawns usually need just 2.5 centimetres of water a week to stay healthy, particularly if they're not cut too short. A frisbee or empty tuna can placed on your lawn will fill up when you've delivered that much water. When mowing, a minimum blade height of 6 to 8 centimetres is generally recommended.

• Plant trees, shrubs and flowers instead of grass. Choose species that are drought tolerant, and you will need much less water through the summer.

• Use a broom instead of water to clean your driveway. Doing so could save you hundreds of litres of water each time.

• If you're washing your car, try a bucket and sponge and not a running hose. Or, a hose with a trigger nozzle can save you buckets of water. Don't use toxic products while washing your car. That water could end up in the nearest river or lake.

• If you have a lake lot, don't destroy any of the natural vegetation in the bed and shore of the lake. Plants filter any water that may be running down from your lot. Also, don't use pesticides and fertilizers if you have a lawn. The fertilizer will contribute to algal blooms in the lake, and the pesticide could harm sensitive aquatic organisms.

Of course there are countless other water-saving ideas out there, some of which might be unique to where you live. Further inspiration and ideas can be drawn from the few intrepid souls who have aspired in recent years to get by on just 25 litres of water a day—one-thirteenth the water that an average Canadian uses. The Water Conservation Challenge began in 2009 when Winnipeger Kevin Freedman challenged himself to use no more than 25 litres of water per day for an entire month. That amount included water to drink, cook with, shower in, wash clothes, flush the toilet, brush teeth, wash dishes, wash hands and so on. His goal was to stay both healthy and hygienic throughout the month-long experiment, and he succeeded.

In 2010, a few others tried to duplicate his achievement. The project involves a lot of sponge baths and creative capture and reuse of water, especially for flushing toilets. At the beginning of her 31 days, Saskatoon resident Alina Siegfried reported what she called "auto-pilot-turning-on-the-tap incidents," a habit likely common to many Canadians. Soon enough, though, she was able to "bank" unused water. "Actually, in truth this challenge has been a lot easier than I thought—and once you make the big changes such as using greywater to flush and bathing out of a bucket, it is not difficult at all to come in under 25 litres of water per day," she wrote in her blog.

What Communities Are Doing

Conserving Water

Plenty of provinces and communities aren't waiting for the federal government to take the lead and are launching their own best efforts at water conservation. BC's Living Water Smart program involves modernizing the province's water laws. Already, implementation of the program has meant that new water licences are being issued with "fish clauses" that allow the government to ensure fish-friendly water levels in rivers.

The water smart program sets two water-efficiency targets by 2020: water use in BC will be 33 percent more efficient, and 50 percent of new municipal demand will be met by conservation. Aside from the previously mentioned low-flow toilet regulation, the province is counting on consumers choosing other water-efficient appliances once they are labelled. The proposal was endorsed in

2009 by all Canadian premiers, and a national working group was established to develop the program.

Some of the driest areas in the country have also pressed ahead on water conservation, often out of necessity as population growth and production increases push against the boundaries of supply. In interior BC, the South East Kelowna Irrigation District (SEKID) began 2010 with ominously low water levels in its main reservoir—less than a quarter of capacity, and the lowest supply in at least eight years. The previous year was one of the lowest supply years in the district's 89-year history and was supposed to be a one-in-a-hundred-year event.

About 85 percent of the water used in the district is for agricultural irrigation. The district draws its water from reservoirs that are primarily replenished by spring melt of the snow pack in the 65-square-kilometre watershed, says the Policy Research Initiative (PRI), which studied the region. "It is considered highly vulnerable to climate change, which is expected to both reduce the snow pack and increase irrigation water demand."

In 1994, in response to a series of droughts and continuing expansion of the irrigated area, the district began installing water meters and providing irrigators with soil moisture meters, primarily as an educational tool, so irrigators would have a better sense of their own water usage and when irrigation was actually needed, the initiative's report says. The meters were followed in 2000 by a program of charging a flat rate for a basic water allotment and a volumetric rate for water use beyond that allotment. In 2003, the district began charging excess users. The metering and education programs had no real impact, but the impact of the pricing program on water use is quite strong. In fact, water use declined by about 40 percent with the pricing program.

There was also a trend of declining water use per hectare before the metering program began, which was likely owing to more efficient equipment being installed as old equipment needed replacing. The PRI analysts suggest that policies encouraging the adoption of new technologies—for example, regulations limiting the sale of inefficient technology, or subsidies for upgrading before the end of the useful life of older, less efficient technology —may be effective in continuing and perhaps even accelerating this trend.

The district now operates by determining the annual allotment for irrigation in the spring prior to the irrigation season. All land-owners are notified by mail as to how much they're going to get. If a property owner exceeds their allotment, the district can charge for the excess water use or shut off irrigation water altogether. In 2009, 85 percent of growers were able to stay within their allotment. In 2010, the district warned irrigators it would shut off water service to a property once their allotment was reached.

Another potential trouble spot is Calgary, the largest city in one of the most water scarce regions in Canada. The city draws water from the Bow and Elbow rivers, neither of which are particularly large. Given the expected arcs of climate change and population growth, the city needs to do better than a conservation rate of 25 percent, says Natural Resources Canada. A target of 50 percent would allow the freshwater resource to be sustained, the department figures.

The city's current program calls for a "30-in-30 water efficiency goal," which aims to accommodate Calgary's future population growth with the same amount of water removed from the river in 2003. This means reducing per capita water consumption by 30 percent over 30 years. The city says it is relying on the participa-tion of individual Calgarians and businesses to achieve the goal of reducing per capita demand to 350 litres per day by 2033. Current per capita demand is 429 litres per day.

There is still a little bit of low-hanging fruit to be had. For a long time Calgary was notorious for having very little water metering, but the city has steadily chipped away at that obstacle to conservation and now has 83 percent of its residential account metered. By the end of 2014, everyone should be metered.

The city has lofty ambitions for its citizens. "Considering the technology available in residential water-use fixtures, such as low-flow toilets, frontloading washers, low-flow shower heads and faucet aerators, we can estimate that average indoor residential water demand target could be as low as 132 litres per person per day," says the city's 2009 year end water efficiency report. "A recent study of Calgarians whose homes have only low-flow water-use fixtures suggests that residential per capita demand can reach well below 100 lpcd."

Many other cities and towns have introduced water conservation bylaws to suit their circumstances and offer incentives, such as rebates, to residents who switch to low-flow fixtures. Only communities that have adopted even more advanced conservation techniques now stick out as exceptional.

Capturing and Reusing Water

Guelph would qualify as exceptional, for now, as it is looking at a water resource that normally gets little attention in Canada. City staff worked with local home builders and existing homeowners in 2009 and 2010 to install a target of 30 greywater reuse systems in new homes and existing homes for a residential greywater reuse pilot project. The Ontario building code allows greywater to be used only to flush toilets or urinals, or to prime a floor drain in a home. Uses may diversify when the code is updated, though. The homes in the Guelph project collect greywater from household showers and baths, purify the greywater collected, and then use this water to flush toilets. Guelph is emphasizing the importance of maintaining the greywater system, which includes cleaning the system's filter and collection tank and adding chlorine pucks.

Greywater is usually defined as wastewater that comes from sources like sinks, washing machines, showers or other uses, besides toilets. It runs through a separate system of purple pipes, coloured that way to carefully distinguish it from drinkable water.

The pilot project is a bit of a field test for all of Canada, with the Federation of Canadian Municipalities kicking in money to underline its interest in how such a program would work in a city. Guelph hopes the project will lead to a residential greywater reuse rebate program and the installation of 200 residential reuse systems by 2019. BC's provincial government says it is also considering greywater recycling and rainwater harvesting as areas for future changes to its building code.

Other countries might mock us for our timid toe-dipping into greywater reuse. A 2010 study on reuse in suburbs in the Western Sydney region in Australia revealed that about half of those surveyed reused greywater regularly or at some time during the last few years. In fact, Australia's current National Rainwater and Greywater Initiative, which is part of a $12.9 billion Water for the Future plan, is so popular that applicants are being warned about delays in payment. The government is offering rebates of up to $500 for households to install rainwater tanks or greywater systems. And, in an accommodation to a very specific Australian circumstance, surf life-saving clubs can get up to $10,000 to install a rainwater tank or to undertake a larger water-saving project.

Capturing rainwater seems like a logical thing to do in water scarce areas, and it does indeed have a history of thousands of years in the drier parts of the world. It's been a bit slower to catch on in most of Canada, where the majority of us are able to simply turn the tap to get plentiful, clean, cheap water, but as water costs rise and the climate turns drier and/or more erratic in some areas, rainwater use has become more common. Through the ubiquitous rain barrel, which squats unobtrusively under downspouts across the country, homeowners have at their disposal free, non-chlorinated water for their gardens and lawns.

There are plenty of other potential uses for rainwater. In some parts of the world, simple filtering and disinfection, by boiling or using alum and chlorine, makes the water drinkable. A few years ago, I met a couple who lived on an acreage outside of Edmonton. For decades they had collected rainwater from their roof in a cistern under their garage. Debris was filtered out through a pair of old pantyhose. They had the water tested by a public health unit and were told they had the best water in the county. The couple used this water for all of their household needs—drinking, bathing, cooking. It was an amazing example of rainwater's potential.

The key to their success, though, was a hard-core conservation ethic. They simply did not waste water. Showers were intermittent bursts of water, in between soaping and shampoo lathering—not long drawn out steamy affairs. Although this couple denied themselves what many of us may deem necessary luxuries, they were pleased to be self-sufficient when it came to water supply.

There would, of course, be even more benefits from broader use of rainwater, especially in cities. Fewer or smaller dams would need to be built, and flooding risks could be lessened as less water would flow to storm water pipes during heavy rainfalls. Less water in storm sewers would also mean less need to treat storm water. If the water is actually being consumed, it could also offset the need for new or larger drinking water treatment plants.

The same side benefits can be achieved through green roofs, which have a flat surface to capture and use water that would have otherwise been channelled to the storm sewers. Porous pavements, though not yet widely used, reduce storm water runoff by allowing water to be absorbed by the ground below.

The Canadian Mortgage and Housing Corporation published a study in 2009 on rainwater harvesting in Ontario and found that it is both technically and socially feasible. The cost, though, will be a barrier. "For individual homeowners, the cost of purchasing and installing a rainwater harvesting system is several times higher than the current price of water," the report says. There will have to be significant cost reductions for these systems and/or increases in the price of water before this practice becomes economically competitive at the household level, the CMHC concluded.

Another class of water we would normally let slip through our fingers is treated wastewater, not from the individual residential level, but at the final treatment plant level. Normally, this water is treated to meet regulations and then released into rivers and streams, usually from where it was withdrawn in the first place. But in some areas it is starting to be regarded as a resource. The Capital Region District on Vancouver Island, for example, will evaluate if it can recover waste heat from this water and if the water can be used for irrigation, urban or industrial purposes, or to boost wetlands or stream flows.

In Edmonton, the wastewater treatment plant worked out a deal with the nearby Petro-Canada refinery, which needed more water to produce low-sulphur diesel fuels and process different feedstocks. A membrane treatment facility was built to filter out a few more impurities and a pipeline was built. The project participants say the deal means less water needs to be drawn directly from the North Saskatchewan River, and less excess nutrients enter the river through the treated wastewater. There is a tradeoff here, though, as the city would normally return almost all of its water to the river, whereas the refinery, now owned by Suncor, uses some of the water to produce hydrogen. Still, there appears to be great interest on the part of Alberta's environmental regulators and the participants in increasing this reuse of wastewater.

Our Resolve: Ephemeral as Water Vapour or Solid as Ice?

We have plenty of options to conserve and protect our water supplies, but will we reach out and grab those life preservers or will we drown in the oncoming flood of water woes?

There are plenty of Canadians who act as lighthouses on this front, pointing out the many possible rocks we could wreck ourselves on. A number of these water experts gathered in Toronto in November 2008 for a roundtable on freshwater issues. The scientists, water policy advisers, lawyers and environmental activists were part of a continuing program on global issues undertaken by Science for Peace and Canadian Pugwash. These groups advance the cause of peace and look for ways to alleviate the causes of global insecurity, including the crises that would arise from failure to achieve an environmentally sustainable future. Canadian Pugwash is the national affiliate of the Pugwash Conferences on Science and World Affairs, which jointly with its founder, Sir Joseph Rotblat, received the Nobel Peace Prize.

In early 2009, the experts issued a freshwater declaration, calling on the federal, provincial and municipal governments to transcend traditional barriers between their jurisdictions to work together to solve our many water problems. The declaration started out with this warning:

> Freshwater, a critical and limited element, is the very basis of ecosystem health and of Canada's social and economic security. Water sustains life. It has a deeply spiritual association both within and outside of all our religious and aboriginal communities. It defines our national identity. But, Canadians have taken it for granted.
>
> We are noticing changes to this precious natural renewable resource. Freshwater shortages are becoming more common, mighty glaciers are disappearing, and pollution problems are worsening. We see disturbing alterations to the landscapes of our northern regions; lakes

and rivers are polluted or otherwise threatened. The mistreatment of our water resources jeopardizes the health of our citizens, threatens our country's magnificent biodiversity, and places the well-being of our nation at risk. Many aboriginal communities endure conditions of Third-World poverty; their drinking water remains under indefinite boil-water advisories. We fail the test of sustainability by overuse and abuse of freshwater in many regions. In some parts of Canada, natural systems have reached a crossroad, beyond which recovery may not be possible.

We can restore life to our threatened lakes and rivers and groundwater, generate innovative solutions to our water problems, protect the health of our citizens, and build social and economic prosperity, but only on the foundation of healthy functioning freshwater ecosystems.

The group then offered its recommendations, foremost among them that the governments should:

- develop a Canada-wide freshwater strategy

- fund freshwater and wastewater infrastructure, linking it to plans that incorporate conservation, efficiency and innovation

- enable formation of enlightened policy by reinstating scientific research and data collection

- improve and enforce regulatory safeguards

- bring climate change adaptation into the mainstream of water policies

- prohibit bulk water removals from Canada's water basins through binding legislation

- assume Canada's share of the collective global responsibility for equitable access to clean water.

CHAPTER EIGHT

Changing Climate

THE SPRING OF 2010 BEGAN ominously in Alberta. Grass fires broke out in early April in the farmlands around Edmonton. Farmers eyed their dry, dusty fields with despair. A tinder-dry 2009 had left soil moisture at an extreme low—a condition favoured only by the coming season's grasshopper crop. Many ranchers were already down to their last wisps of winter feed for their cattle following an extremely poor year for pasture and hay production. In 2009, more than $54 million in hay and pasture insurance claims were paid out across the province—almost 10 times the amount in the year before.

Environment Canada's meteorologists declared the winter the warmest since nationwide records began in 1948; the national average temperature was 4° C above normal. Overall, the country also experienced its driest winter yet in its 63-year record, at 22 percent below normal. Mother Nature was particularly stingy in parts of Alberta, Saskatchewan and Ontario that received 60 percent less precipitation than normal.

Senior climatologist David Phillips says models are predicting, with high confidence, a warmer than normal summer from coast-to-coast-to-coast. Urban and rural Canadians respond differently to that news, he says. Urbanites consider it good news "because generally people like to drink beer on outdoor patios, and it's good for beaching and tenting and cottaging and things like that." For farmers, it can be both good and bad news. "It's more heat for growing food stuffs. But on the other hand they're going to need more precipitation than they would normally get because there will be greater demands for that moisture from the atmosphere," says Phillips.

Nature always has first dibs, drawing the moisture out from the ground and vegetation before humans can grab it for their various uses, he says. "What we're seeing then with warmer than normal is we would need a wetter than normal summer to be able to match the demands from temperature, let alone what's gone before that."

The various models Environment Canada uses are a lot less confident about precipitation predictions. There is a slight tendency toward a wetter than usual summer in the southern Prairies and Okanagan. But Phillips doesn't find it confidence boosting, especially given the ultra-dry conditions from the previous two years in some of the Prairie regions.

Edmonton and the surrounding area were particularly hard hit, he says. Phillips surveyed the city's records going back to the 1880s, and nowhere did he find two drier back-to-back years than 2008 and 2009. Indeed, the city's arborists declared the spring of 2010 a season of do-or-die: it was either going to rain lots, or the thousands of trees suffering from years of below normal moisture were finally going to succumb. It's an unfortunate situation, but Phillips says it might help rural people. When drought becomes an urban issue, then people wake up, politicians wake up, and they realize what farmers are complaining about.

Few people have Phillips' perspective and access to data, though. And what he sees might surprise many. "1998 in Edmonton was the last year that there was a wetter than normal year," he says. "In any decade that you look at, typically what you see, if I look at 100 years—10 decades—I can guarantee you that in every decade there are some wet years and there are some dry years. Now if you have more dry years than wet years then it's probably declared a dry decade. Clearly what we've seen since

1999, 11 years, is not one of those years in Edmonton was wetter than normal. Every one was drier than normal."

The New Normal

The persistent dryness of the century's first decade is not normal—at least not to the people who settled in the Prairies in the last 150 years. "Climatologists will tell you that one of the things about the 20th century was it was a humid century. We didn't have back-to-back-to-back droughts. We had maybe back-to-back; we had a tough decade in the '30s." Even in the 1930s, though, they at least had some soil moisture recharge in the cold season. "True, the growing season was bone dry. But then what you had was some restoration or recovery or restoring of the soil moisture through either a wet fall or wet spring or a wet winter." But these days, what we're seeing is year-round drought or dryness, which is different than what we've seen before, he added.

People need to wake up to this new normal, says Phillips, who likes to use the analogy of withdrawing money from your bank balance. "If you make no deposits, eventually you're going to have to declare bankruptcy. And what we're doing is, nature is withdrawing, and so are human beings. It's become a vital resource for so many things that we do. We've been overusing that water. It's like a drunken sailor, spending that resource. And yet we know it's not restoring itself. It's not being put back in."

When climatologists refer to "normals" in an area, whether it be temperature or precipitation, they follow the global convention of averaging weather from a previous 30-year block. So our current normals are averages of what occurred during 1971 to 2000. Usually, when the oldest decade is dropped and the newest adopted, the kind of changes you see are a fraction of a degree or a couple of millimetres, Phillips says. "My sense is, adding the 10 years from the 2000 decade will probably change the normal more significantly than we've ever seen before in Canada." There are a few reasons for that change: the lower amounts of precipitation on the Prairies; a dramatic temperature change in the last 10 years in the Maritimes; and the shedding of the 1970s, which was a cold and snowy decade for Canada, Phillips explains.

It's important for people to realize that we've shifted away from our old "normal" climate experience, Phillips says. "Particularly in more rural areas and more frontier areas, you come to depend upon the weather you expect. And when you don't get the weather you expect, then there are clear issues."

Phillips has been a climatologist for 40 years, and for 35 of those years he has always used the past as a guide to the future. This practice is the governing principle of being what he calls an applied climatologist, someone who provides information to people who are "designing homes and curling rinks and growing food stuffs and planning reservoirs and planting trees for the next generation, all those things that we do with climate in mind." In the past we've always used the longest period of record that we can find, he explains. "Because when you look in the past, the 150 years, the past is telling you what you're going to see in the future. Buried in that 150 years is the hundred-year event, the storm of the century."

That principle doesn't hold anymore, though. "When it comes to these tactical kind of decisions, like what crop to grow, what water should I let out of a reservoir, or how much water we need for irrigation, or for forest fire fighting, or things we plan on a day-to-day or month-to-month kind of basis, then I sometimes think we mask the outcome based on the longer period record. That's why I say when farmers say to me, 'What should I grow this year?' I say, 'Well don't do what your parents did or what your teachers told you to do because the climate has changed.'"

Another huge issue is the new variability of the weather. "Sometimes the driest and wettest [year] is within the last 10 years...

There's no such thing as the norm anymore. What we've come to expect is the unexpected."

And the extremity of the weather is another factor. In recent years, sudden deluges have swamped cities across the country, causing flooding and extensive damage to homes and streets. City planners face the prospect that the storm water systems they've built in past decades are no longer capable of handling these freak storms, which somehow are becoming more run-of-the-mill. Homeowners who were allowed to build in flood plains are also at greater risk. "My concern is the fact that what we're seeing is more of these 'storms of the century,'" says Phillips. "How many storms of the century can you live through? You should see one, if you're lucky. But now what we're seeing is a multitude of them.

"It's almost as if any wild card or joker in the weather deck is there and whatever we turn over shouldn't shock us. But boy, when you've based everything on normal, it throws you way off. And I think that that's really what I think is happening, is that we're puzzled more by it. It's causing us more grief, more expense, because [the weather is] not behaving the way our grandparents and our teachers told us...it would be."

Adapting to Climate Change

If climate change is going to continue treating the Prairies like a punching bag, it helps to have a hint about the coming heft of those shots so that we can adapt. Already, annual temperatures have increased 1.4° C in Canada, Statistics Canada reported in 2008. Temperature increases are greatest in the Yukon and North British Columbia Mountains region and the Mackenzie District of the Northwest Territories, the report noted.

Changes on the Prairies

Concerns about climate change are especially high in the Prairies, which appear to be at the centre of the coming water scarcity vortex. "Seasonal water deficits occur in all regions of Canada, but only in the Prairies can precipitation cease for more than a month, surface waters disappear for entire seasons, and water deficits persist for a decade or more, putting landscapes at risk of desertification," wrote lead authors Dave Sauchyn and Suren Kulshreshtha in the Prairies subsection of the federal climate change and adaptation report released in 2008. "The Prairies are Canada's major dryland," they point out. "Recent trends and future projections include lower summer stream flows, falling lake levels, retreating glaciers, and increasing soil- and surface-water deficits. A trend of increased aridity will most likely be realized through a greater frequency of dry years." This is a serious concern because, as they put it: "The most costly climate events in Canadian history have been droughts on the Prairies."

Research shows that the picture in the headwaters of the major Prairie rivers is already changing rapidly. "The glacier area of the Rockies is actually quite small and getting smaller," says John Pomeroy, Canada Research Chair in Water Resource and Climate Change at the University of Saskatchewan. He and a team of researchers are learning as much as they can about the hydrology of Canada's high altitude and high latitude places. Their program is called Improving Processes and Parameterization for Prediction in Cold Regions, or IP3 for short.

"The South Saskatchewan River basin has lost about 35 percent of its area in the last 25 years of the 20th century. And the North Saskatchewan basin has lost about 22 percent of its area in the same time. As a result the glacier contribution to stream flow is less than six percent for the North and South Saskatchewan rivers. In fact, for the South Saskatchewan basin when you look at Calgary and places like that, it's down to about one percent, two percent."

Prairie residents might be surprised to hear glaciers are contributing that little to the rivers' flows. Pomeroy and his team of research colleagues have found that the majority of the water actually comes from snowmelt and rainfall. But this isn't good news. In fact, there's bad news about the glaciers and then there's bad news about snowfall. "The thing to remember about a glacier is that when a glacier is sort of healthy, not growing or shrinking, it's not contributing any water to stream flow on an annual basis," Pomeroy says. "Its ice mass isn't changing from year to year. Therefore the glacier contribution to stream flow comes from a reduction in this mass of ice. If it's not shrinking, it's not contributing. So this percentage is from the shrinkage from the glaciers. In fact, it's kind of high. Six percent is scary."

Pomeroy adds that the timing of the glacier contribution to flow is very important. "It tends to occur in late summer and early fall when other stream flow components are small. That tends to be a very dry period in the Rockies. The snow pack is gone and often there's not much rain. If you remember last September [in 2009], it was bone dry in the Rockies. Glaciers were melting rapidly. So a lot of the stream flow we saw then was glacier melt."

Of the 853 glaciers that were inventoried in 1975 in the North Saskatchewan and South Saskatchewan river basins, 328 have disappeared completely, according to Statistics Canada. So it looks like the major glacier ice contribution to stream flow has already occurred, Pomeroy says. Each year, the contributions are getting smaller. "So we're basically relying on snowmelt and rainfall now for generating our stream flow."

There's a problem with that reliance. "There's been a decline in the snow cover period in the southern Rockies in southern Alberta of around a month since the early 1970s." What used to fall as snow in May, maybe June and even July, is coming as rain now at high elevations, Pomeroy explains. In the Bow River this shows up as higher flows earlier in the season. "And as a result there's less snowmelt water for late flows. So the August flows are down 25 percent over the last century. That's a big one."

This reduction means that rivers need to be managed differently, he adds. "Our management system has had very little storage in it because we've been relying on the high mountain snow pack to capture nine months of precipitation and then release it right up until about July and then have the glaciers kick in in late July and August to cover the rest. And we've been quite fortunate in that we often get pretty wet weather in spring and early summer in the Rockies, so that kind of covers the rest. So now we've got less snowfall, and earlier snowmelt and a smaller glacier contribution. So it makes us very reliant upon spring rains to keep our rivers up in the summer period when we're using water for irrigation, hydroelectric and urban water supply. And it makes us more vulnerable to drought, because in the previous drought years the snow pack might be small, and the rains might not come, but the glaciers would melt rapidly. We just don't have that protection anymore." Statistics Canada emphasized the tightening supplies in a 2010 report. The renewable freshwater per unit area of the Prairies is less than that for either Australia or South Africa, they said. "From 1971 to 2004, the water yield for the Prairies fell by 0.56 cubic kilometres a year. In perspective, this annual loss represents about 80 percent of the total volume of water that was produced by drinking water plants in this region in 2005."

Pomeroy says there are plenty of management options—and many of them are bad. "There are a lot of lessons out there on things not to do, but not a lot of lessons on what to do to make it exactly right." A visitor from Spain told him about the situation there. "The Pyrenees in northern Spain is a lot like southern Alberta. They've put dams everywhere, hundreds of dams. Their stream flow is down 70 percent. Their glaciers are pretty well gone. They're farther down the road than we are, and it's not very nice."

And it's not working for the people there, he says. "In the big cities, the water is almost undrinkable. They've hit the limits.

They've totally given up on the fish in the rivers and streams. And they're just trying to keep water going to the irrigation and into the cities. This visitor described this stuff in detail and I thought, 'Wow, we don't want that here.'"

Changes in the North

Farther north, near Fort Simpson, NWT, another of Pomeroy's IP3 colleagues, Bill Quinton, is witnessing rapid landscape change brought on by permafrost melt. "The landscape there is quite flat," explains Pomeroy. "And it's a series of peat plateaus, which are well-drained forests. But the black spruce forest is sitting on ice ridge permafrost. It's about half ice. In between these peat plateaus are areas without permafrost that are open fens. These are open swamps; they don't have trees. The landscape is kind of a pattern of these raised plateaus and then fens in between them. What's happening is the ice is melting very quickly there. I think the number is around one-third that he's measured of the melt out of the area of these plateaus since the 1940s. A lot of it has been quite rapid, in the last 10 years in fact. When the ice melts out the trees collapse; they fall over. The level of the land drops quite a bit, such that it gets flooded and the area becomes a swamp. So it's a big change. And a terrible place to try to build a pipeline."

There is not much stability there, Pomeroy says. "It's becoming unrecognizable within a human's lifetime." Pomeroy has looked at aerial photos from 1947 of the southern NWT. "By comparing it with those, you can see that what were tiny lakes are now big lakes. And what were once big black spruce forests are now swamp," he says.

Still farther north, the team has been looking at the hydrology along the northern tree line, north of Inuvik. Instead of trees taking root farther north, as many people would expect, the already-present shrubs are increasing in height, Pomeroy says. "As they increase in height they trap snow on the ground that would normally be blowing around in Arctic blizzards. When it blows around a fair amount of it sublimates, we figure one-third, so it goes back into water vapour. The part of the blowing snow that doesn't sublimate ends up in large drifts near the streams, and these drifts hang on into late summer, sometimes right through the summer, and contribute to stream flow throughout the summer."

But that doesn't happen when the shrubs get taller. "The atmosphere in the winter sees the shrub instead of the snow," says Pomeroy. "And the shrubs will warm up in the sun in the spring and become quite warm and quite dark. This is an albedo feedback to the atmosphere which creates further warming in the springtime. Also the shrubs hold the snow in place so it doesn't sublimate, it's deeper all over the tundra, and it provides greater insulation all over the tundra, which means the soils start to become warmer. So we think in time this may contribute to permafrost thaw, though we haven't seen this yet. But we think it's going to be a contributing factor."

Pomeroy says a lot of the tundra lakes are actually held together by the permafrost. When it melts, the lakes drain and disappear. That water goes to the Arctic Ocean, meaning greater freshwater flows into the ocean and less water on northern landscapes.

All of this change is happening so quickly that it knocks the step-like process of scientific knowledge accumulation off balance. Of the northern landscape, Pomeroy says, "It's changing rapidly. It's tough to keep up with, and there's so much going on. We're just figuring out how it functions in a natural sense, and then at the same time we have to figure out how it's changing."

John Smol has watched the changing climate pull its Houdini-like tricks on northern waterbodies, too. Only he knows it's not magic that's behind the disappearing act—it's a collective act of humanity. Smol has spent 27 years, more than half of his life, working in the High Arctic. There, on Ellesmere Island, he monitored

40 ponds, some as big as a football field, others the size of a house. Fossils in the sediment of those ponds showed that changes started happening about 100 years ago, he says. "The High Arctic is the first to show signs of climate change to the most degree because of feedback mechanisms. So we've seen tremendous changes up there."

In the 1990s, Smol and his colleagues predicted some of the ponds would dry up completely. They were right about that, but wrong about how long it would take. Several of the ponds, which fossil records showed were permanent waterbodies since the last ice age, dried up completely for the first time in 2005 and again in 2006—and some as early into the season as early July. "We had predicted it would happen based on our paleo work, but we didn't think it would happen so quickly," he says. "That's the thing about the Arctic, everything is happening far more quickly than we thought it would be."

Smol says it was depressing to see the ponds gone. "It was like your friends have disappeared. I'd been monitoring them since my twenties."

Unlike the waterbodies farther west that were draining because of melting permafrost, these ponds were underlain by granitic bedrock. The culprit here was the same—climate change—it was just using a more common mechanism—evaporation. The key factor was the amount of time the ponds were ice free, says Smol. "The amount of time they're ice free has greatly increased, and that's why we think they're evaporating away. When I used to go up there in the early 1980s, they were just opening up sometimes in late June, early July. And they were already sometimes totally covered by snow by late August, early September." Now, Smol's instruments tell him that sometimes they're opening up as early as May.

Not only does this longer ice-free period cause the water to evaporate away, sometimes completely, but it also makes all the ponds saltier. "I use the analogy of putting a pot of soup on the stove and taking the lid off," explains Smol. "It's much like a pond under extended heat or more heat. If you watch your soup, the soup level keeps going down. Well that's exactly what happened to the ponds. We watched them slowly decrease in water level. If you keep tasting the soup it gets saltier and saltier. That's because the water's evaporated away and the salt's left behind. I was measuring the salinity of these ponds going back to 1983, and I could show a steady increase in salinity." Increased salinity kills off or deforms all but a few organisms. One pond's assemblage of aquatic invertebrates consisted almost entirely of fairy shrimp the day before it dried up.

"A key 'tipping point' has now been passed: Arctic ponds that were permanent waterbodies for millennia are now ephemeral," wrote Smol and co-author Marianne Douglas in their 2007 paper on their research. "The ecological ramifications of these changes are likely severe, and will cascade throughout the Arctic ecosystem (e.g., waterfowl habitat and breeding grounds, invertebrate population dynamics and food for insectivores, drinking water for animals, etc.). Furthermore, lower water levels will have many indirect environmental effects, such as further concentration of pollutants. Ironically, High Arctic ponds, which are such important bellwethers of environmental change, are now disappearing because of climatic warming."

The changes have many practical implications for humans, too. The federal report on climate change and adaptation points to some key changes that people will need to make in northern Canada: existing infrastructure will require repairs and engineering modifications to deal with permafrost warming and thaw; reliance on ice routes will need to shift to open-water or land-based transport systems; and hydroelectricity generators will need to adapt to changes in the timing of river flows.

Changes Elsewhere in Canada

In Atlantic Canada, coastal communities face saltwater intrusion in their groundwater supply as sea level rises and more storm events of an increasingly intense nature cause storm surges, coastal erosion and flooding. Drier summers could mean a squeeze on water resources, which would affect municipal water supplies and challenge a range of sectors, including agriculture, fisheries, tourism and energy, the federal report predicts. "Re-examination of cropping systems and improved water management would help the agricultural sector to adapt, although non-climatic factors, such as socioeconomic and demographic trends, may limit adaptive responses."

In Quebec, extreme weather events associated with climate change are believed to pose increased risks in the south subregion to the province's aging infrastructure, vulnerable populations and communities living in areas exposed to natural hazards. Milder winters and hotter, more humid summers could exacerbate water-use conflicts and lead to further degradation and loss of wetlands that rely on flooding.

Severe weather is also a big concern in Ontario, where flooding associated with unusually fierce storms has disrupted transportation and communication lines. One particularly ferocious line of severe thunderstorms on an August day in 2005 inflicted more than $500 million worth of damage. "Lengthy and extensive power outages have resulted from the failure of transmission grids and distribution lines," the report says. Water levels in the Great Lakes are also a focus of interest. "Projected decreases in Great Lakes water levels may compromise shipping and reduce hydroelectricity output by more than 1100 megawatts," the report says. Also, water shortages, already documented in southern regions of the province, are projected to become more frequent as summer temperatures and evaporation rates increase. "Sections of Durham County, Waterloo and Wellington Counties, and the shoreline of southern Georgian Bay, where growth strategies indicate that the population will continue to increase significantly, will become more vulnerable to shortages within the next 20 years."

BC is heavily reliant on hydroelectric power generation, which accounts for nearly 90 percent of the power supply. Adaptation will involve managing electricity demands, which are expected to increase by 30 to 60 percent by 2025, and updating power-generating infrastructure. Small hydro and "run of river" alternatives can increase capacity, but they are more vulnerable to variable river flows than are facilities with large storage reservoirs.

The province also faces some of the same issues as the Prairies: smaller glaciers and declining snow pack, along with shifts in timing and amount of precipitation, and prolonged drought will increasingly limit water supply during periods of peak demand, the report predicts. Increasing demand for irrigation will have to compete with other water uses, especially in areas of high population growth. Competition among water uses will increase and have implications for transborder agreements.

Water Scarcity and Related Potential Threats

Irrigation Appropriation and Contamination of Water

Bob Sandford thinks agricultural water use will cause strain far beyond quantity issues. Sandford is a water expert who began his career as an innovative interpreter with Parks Canada. He has worked hard to have people understand the ecology and human history of the Rocky Mountains. But Sandford himself would tell you that his most significant work is raising awareness about the state and management of freshwater in Canada.

He began this work in 2002, when he was Canadian chair of the United Nations International Year of Mountains. The focus sharpened in 2003–2004 when he took on the role of Canadian chair of the UN International Year of Fresh Water and Wonder of Water Initiative. Now, he is Canada's chairman of the UN Water for Life Decade, which stretches to 2015. In addition, he is part of so many water organizations it's hard to keep track of them all.

Sandford's concerns about water use in agriculture run particularly deep. He thinks agricultural water use is becoming a global issue. "It's becoming an issue because contemporary industrial-scale food production practices inevitably result in reduced return flows to nature of water of poor quality, which diminished and often water-starved natural aquatic ecosystems no longer have the capacity to purify. So we're wiping out wetlands and then we're also loading the remaining agricultural return flows with nutrients and pesticide residues. And natural systems are no longer able to deal with this. And therefore we're getting eutrophication of lakes. And we're getting tremendous damage to such things as Lake Winnipeg and huge dead zones in the Gulf of Mexico."

He continues, "Here's my prediction: I think within five years, agricultural water contamination is going to be recognized nationally as one of our most serious water issues."

And he isn't afraid to raise the warning among farmers. Sandford, who is a popular guest speaker, told agriculture representatives at a conference in early 2010 that they better get on top of this issue, or their social licence to operate in some sectors of agriculture will probably be challenged. "You can increase your productivity through your agricultural practices, but in the end what does that do if it destroys your water resources and you absolutely have to effectively treat water every time that you're going to use it? This is the sort of situation that is a nightmare for me, where you end up with nature and all of humanity effectively on dialysis because you can't drink the water anywhere because it's been contaminated by some sort of use. And the only water you can drink of course has been treated. This is the way we're moving here in southern Canada."

On top of concerns about fertilizers and pesticides tainting the water, Sandford also thinks too much water is being dedicated to agricultural use. Right now irrigation districts have rights to

70 percent of the water allocations in southern Alberta, he says. Many of these licences are senior, meaning they got them first, long before other licences were handed out to towns and industries. In Alberta, the system still operates under the "first in time, first in right" system (FITFIR). Irrigators and other people with those rights are standing fiercely by this setup, says Sandford. In a drought, they can even legally deny towns and cities around them the drinking water they need for survival, though he doubts that would happen.

There is movement to make irrigation systems more efficient. In Alberta, the provincial government and the irrigation districts have been chipping away at making water distribution more efficient through their 8000 kilometres of conveyance systems and 725,000 hectares of irrigated land. They've improved over 50 percent of the conveyance systems since the Irrigation Rehabilitation Program began in the late 1960s, according to the government. To date, the combined rehabilitation contribution of the Alberta government and Irrigation District water users totals approximately $665 million. The province's latest budget shows another $72 million earmarked for irrigation rehabilitation grants over the next three years.

Potential water savings are huge. One Alberta irrigation group, the Western Irrigation District, notes that switching from wheel-move and high-pressure centre-pivot irrigation systems to more energy efficient centre-pivot irrigation systems could save 250,000 to 850,000 litres of water per hectare per year.

This district says it is aggressively rehabilitating its water delivery system. That includes replacing smaller canals with PVC pipe to eliminate water loss from evaporation and seepage, and cleaning larger canals to reduce siltation and improve water quality. The district also acknowledges that since the government shut down new allocations from the Bow River it will have the task, as a senior licence holder, of sharing its supply with new customer demand. Some of those demands are expected to come from nearby urban expansion.

The Eastern Irrigation District made a move to sell some its allocation in early 2010. Its application to the government asked for permission to amend its water licence so it could provide six billion litres of water for municipal, agricultural, commercial, industrial, habitat enhancement and recreational purposes. An Alberta water protection group called Water Matters criticized the application, saying it would effectively make the district a water broker. The government could hamper its own forthcoming review of its water allocation system, the group said, if it approved the application because current legislation has not prioritized water for basic human needs and healthy rivers. The district's proposed amendment does not guarantee the water will remain a public good with public oversight, Water Matters said. In addition, they worry that being able to sell water rights will encourage the district to use more water, an important consideration given the area is already under significant water scarcity pressure. Irrigation districts don't use all the water they've been allocated; the Eastern Irrigation District averages 74 percent.

Sandford thinks reforming FITFIR water allocation structures is really important. He doesn't think there's a water scarcity issue in the South Saskatchewan River basin, but a licensing problem. And it's not just the irrigators that have overly fat allocations. He says Calgary also has a huge senior water licence that gives priority access to far more water than it currently needs. Surrounding communities aren't happy that Calgary has corralled so much of the regional water when they are already at or near the limits of their existing water licences, he says. This situation is a setup for challenges and conflicts, and a reform of water allocation rights is needed to prevent that, he adds.

In his book *Restoring the Flow*, Sandford wrote about the increasingly tight water supplies in Spain and how the federal government there spent billions of dollars upgrading the irrigation systems. And yet, irrigators will not give any of their water savings back so that the water can be used for other purposes, which has caused resentment. Water scarcity invariably attracts public attention to heavy water users, he wrote. "In the last decade the notion that farmers [in Spain] use excessive amounts of water because it is sold to them so cheaply that there is no incentive to use it more sparingly has become deeply ingrained in the public imagination."

Sandford also writes, "If we can learn anything from Spain it may be that we should expect a great deal of tension between big cities and the irrigation agriculture community if such circumstances come to be."

And it isn't that unlikely. "You have to think in the long term," Sandford says. "There are two things that are really deeply troubling here that we need to pay attention to that form the foundation of our vulnerability. We've grown our population and our economic development right to the limits of our water supply. That's our *current* water supply." He says that if you look at lingering vulnerabilities, one the of problems is the natural variability within climate circumstances in the Great Plains.

Sandford points to research by Sauchyn that shows droughts in previous centuries were much longer than anything in the instrumental record. "We can't survive a two-year drought without tremendous anxiety and billions of dollars of economic impact," Sandford says. "How are we going to survive a decade-long drought?" If drought becomes a more common and persistent feature in the Prairies then we are really in trouble, Sandford believes. Part of preparing for this possibility includes setting proper priorities, he says.

Lorne Taylor, a former Alberta environment minister and architect of the province's Water for Life strategy, agrees something needs to be done and that FITFIR isn't working very well anymore. "You've got a lot of old water licences that don't use their allocation," says Taylor one sunny day from the 24th floor of an office tower with a view of the North Saskatchewan River. "So the question is: what is the mechanism that causes that water to be put into some kind of productive cycle?"

Taylor soaked up his water ethics at an early age. His father ran a cattle ranch in southeastern Alberta, traditionally a water-short area. "I remember being on the ranch with him in the midst of a hot summer—I don't know what month but it was hot, I can remember that because we didn't have air conditioning—and him worrying out loud to himself cuz his dugout was dry and we had cow-calf pairs in that field. And he was wondering out loud, I don't know what his exact words were, but he was saying, 'Where am I going to move these cow-calf pairs to because all our dugouts are dry?' And a five-year-old, watching this, you could see your dad was worried and that made a huge impression on me."

In Medicine Hat, where he grew up, water restrictions were the norm. You could only water your lawns and gardens on either odd days or even days, he recalls. "And if somehow you forgot, your neighbour would come and knock on your door and say, 'Mrs. Taylor, this is not an odd day. It's not your watering time.' And it was very community centred. My mom would go and knock on somebody's door and say, 'Mrs. X, you're on even.' And they'd immediately say, 'Oh, sorry, sorry, we forgot.'"

Taylor is now chairman of the Alberta Water Resources Institute. Ever a staunch Conservative, he is sensitive to how people feel about something they perceive as their property, even when it comes to water rights. "If you've got a licence and you've got a lot more water than you're using, do you want me to come and say to you, 'Guess what, you can't have all that water anymore'? Can you imagine the controversy? So allocation is vital. So how do we make it attractive for you to say, 'OK, Lorne, you can have that water'?... How do we make it attractive to the city of Calgary to give water even to the surrounding communities? That's a huge allocation issue."

One of the grating factors in Spain is that irrigators are still using the water from their upgraded, expensive systems to grow low-value crops, Sandford says. Taylor, who toured Spain with Sandford, agrees this is a problem. "My own personal opinion," and not one of the institute, Taylor stresses, "is you should not be growing forage crops with expensive water and irrigated land." He doesn't have a problem with farmers using "extra" water achieved from conservation efforts for more production, as long as it doesn't get in the way of achieving the other goals of the Water for Life "triumvirate"—safe drinking water and healthy ecosystems, in addition to the sustainable economy.

What we actually need to do is stop compartmentalizing all the different uses of water and begin to think of the resource more holistically. "Right now, I think we have a too-atomized approach to water," says Sandford. "Everybody who needs it uses it on their terms. In the future we're going to have to think hydrologically."

Sandford says we tend to think of water as an independent substance and we separate it from land. "What I think the new ethic is going to do is define and allow us to clearly operate within a different interface. And that will be the land, life, water, weather, climate interface. So instead of thinking of those things as separate elements, we're going to have to think of all of those elements together and how we can create and live within the sustainable interaction of all of those."

Change to our approach in water management isn't happening fast enough for either Taylor or Sandford. The drought that ushered in the 21st century in Alberta helped Taylor get the political and public support to create the Water for Life strategy in 2003, but when the drought subsided a bit the urgency seemed to drain out of the project. Now, with the last couple of years of bone dry conditions again in parts of Alberta, there could be renewed pressure.

But Sandford is frustrated by that short-sightedness. "Do we have to have farmer suicides every three days before we finally get to understand that we've got to think this way? It seems to take an emergency for these things to finally reach the level of public policy concern that somebody does something about it." Sandford says the technology already exists to deal with water scarcity. "All sorts of innovations exist. Watershed basin councils exist. They know the threats. But our governments do not seem to want to change their habits, practices or policies in order to respond to this. There is too much attention on other issues at the moment. And that's why this vulnerability grows silently every day to a pretty obvious, likely outcome."

Thirsty Neighbours

Climate change isn't impacting just Canada, obviously. The Americans are feeling it, too. Atmospheric researchers located at the University of California at San Diego call water shortages the "new normal." In 2008, an analysis led by the university's Scripps Institution of Oceanography showed that climate change is already disrupting water supplies in the western United States. "Trends in snowpack, river runoff and air temperatures—three fundamental indicators of the status of the West's hydrological cycle—point to a decline in the region's most valuable natural resource, water, as population and demand grows in the West," the institution said.

Although the western states are often seen at the focus of water crises, they are far from alone. The U.S. Government Accountability Office surveyed water managers in each of the states in 2003. Of the 47 that responded (California, New Mexico and Michigan were silent), 36 states said that even under normal conditions, freshwater shortages are anticipated in localities, regions or state-wide in the next 10 years. The GAO said the consequences may be severe.

Maude Barlow, national chairperson of the Council of Canadians, points to this growing scarcity with concern. "It's not like it's just a situational or small kinds of parts of the United States that are in trouble," she says. "They're continuing, like we are, to use water as if there's no tomorrow." There are areas of the U.S. where the water wall has already been hit, she adds, including huge parts of California and all of the states that are dependent on either the snowmelt of the Rockies or the Colorado River.

As the problem grows, so will the number of Americans looking north for salvation. Barlow, who served as senior adviser on water to the president of the UN General Assembly in 2008–2009, believes there is willingness on both sides of the border to move water from Canada to the U.S., despite a prohibitive cost. "You know, people used to say the tar sands were too expensive, they would never amount to a major export," she reflects. "I can remember that. People say it's too expensive to ship this water. Well, maybe, except if you're out. And then nothing's too expensive. Then you do what you have to do. So I do believe the pressure will continue to mount over time. But I don't think it will all come from the States. I think it's going to come from business people here in Canada."

A film released in 2010 called *Water on the Table* explores this issue. The movie, directed by Liz Marshall, follows Barlow around for a year as she travels through the U.S. and Canada, promoting water as a human right, and not a commodity. One voice in the film is Marcel Boyer, senior economist and president of the Montreal Economic Institute, which in 2009 released a report on the possibilities of cashing in on Quebec water. "The Maude Barlows of the world see the business of water as part of a huge international conspiracy of governments and big corporations who are trying to exploit the people," he says in the film. "This is how these people see it. There are no facts to back this up."

In late July 2010, the United Nations General Assembly actually voted in favour of a resolution recognizing access to clean drinking water and sanitation as a human right. It passed by a vote of 122 in favour with none against. However, there were 41 abstentions, including Canada.

The debate over exporting large quantities of northern Quebec water has never really taken place, wrote Pierre Gingras, an industrial engineer and associate researcher with the institute:

> The only minimally detailed proposal that was ever discussed was that of the so-called 'GRAND Canal' first made in the 1960s then revived by a group of business people in the 1980s.

> It was a grandiose project, along the scale of the pyramids of Giza, involving the construction of a massive dam closing James Bay and a long canal diverting the accumulated freshwater to the Great Lakes. Several nuclear power plants would have been required just to pump the water, and the cost of the project at the time was estimated at $100 billion, which would be $175 billion today— three times the annual budget of the entire Quebec government!

> What has always been missing to allow for a proper rational discussion of this opportunity was a technically realistic, sustainable plan to develop the resource, a project that doesn't involve massive changes to the ecosystem and that would be financially viable.

His paper summarizes such a project, which they called the Northern Waters complex. Gingras proposes capturing the seasonal runoff from three rivers in the James Bay basin that have not yet been developed for hydroelectric power: the Broadback, Waswanipi and Bell. These "surplus waters" would then be diverted via the natural riverbeds through a series of six pumping stations along the Bell River up to the Val d'Or pass, which is the highest point, before the waters can flow by gravity down the Ottawa River valley. This would allow an additional average flow of 800 cubic metres of water per second (CMS) to flow into the Ottawa River down to the Saint Lawrence just above Montreal. Gingras calculated that the project, with the addition of a few more power facilities, would produce more than 14 terawatt hours of net energy annually. But the main benefit would be the export of a large quantity of freshwater without one drop having to leave the province, he wrote.

The flow of 800 CMS from an alternative source into the Saint Lawrence River would theoretically reduce the amount of water required from the Great Lakes by the equivalent. This water could then be used to regulate the level of the Saint Lawrence River and Great Lakes, which has been dropping in recent years. Or, Gingras proposed, Ontarians and Americans could choose to use a certain quantity for their freshwater consumption needs. The surplus could be delivered to the Midwest and South via a detour through the Chicago Canal and Mississippi River. Altogether, this water could theoretically serve the needs of 150 million people, he says.

Gingras estimated it would cost about $15 billion in current dollars at the end of 2022, when the project would be completed. He estimates Quebec could make about $2 billion annually selling the energy and $20 billion annually for the 25 billion cubic metres of water that would be diverted.

Former Environment Canada water policy adviser Frank Quinn publicly criticized the proposal in the *National Post*. He pointed out that there has been a lot of dispute between Illinois and the other Great Lakes states and provinces about the Chicago diversion at different points in time. The matter ended up before the U.S. Supreme Court, which capped the diversion rate in 1967 at 91 CMS. It's not logical to think the other Great Lakes jurisdictions would approve several times that amount flowing out of the basin. "That's the very thing they would never agree to," he says, especially now that the eight states have a compact that officially protects their waters from removal.

The issue is likely to linger, though. "I think you can be sure the topic will never disappear, just because who knows about the future," Quinn says. "We are going to have enduring growth in population, and so many people want to live in the American Southwest. If you don't think too much about it, it looks obvious

—it's going to have to happen. But when you look into who's for it, who's against it and why and some of the other calamities we've gotten into with big diversions of water within Canada we don't want to repeat those kinds of mistakes forever. And we don't want to get tangled up in a project where we would be the exporter, supplying a mighty power; you better be careful what you're doing because you can't change your mind after getting into it and it's too late."

Herb Gray, a former Liberal MP who wrapped up an eight-year term as Canadian chairman of the International Joint Commission in January 2010, concurs with Quinn, that nobody around the Great Lakes is interested in seeing any export of water from the Great Lakes. "There's no surplus," he says. "Only one percent a year is restored by snowmelt and rain, and all the water is actually being used either for sewage treatment or drinking water or industry or recreational boating or shipping or hydropower. If you look at the water you don't see that all going on, but it's all being used."

Gray says there is no current project being raised in Congress or the U.S. administration for accessing boundary waters. He takes comfort in the fact that there is a Canadian federal law banning export of water from the Canadian side of any international basin and that there are equivalent provincial regulations in Ontario and Quebec. "And in the U.S. there's this compact, so the Great Lakes states, supported by the federal government, are of the same mind as their Canadian counterparts." Then he adds, "We have to be vigilant, of course."

Alien Invaders

On some issues, the barricade of vigilance was set up a little late. The most recent report on the state of the Great Lakes tallies 185 aquatic and 157 terrestrial non-native species in the basin.

"Each new non-native species can interact with the ecosystem in unpredictable ways, with at least 10 percent of non-native species considered to be invasive, meaning that they negatively impact ecosystem health," the report says.

Also called alien species, they've made their way into the area in a multitude of ways. Many were stowaways in the ballast carried by large ships, which emptied that water into the lakes. Some also hitched rides on the hulls of these ships. Zebra mussels are thought to have chosen this route to the lakes in the late 1980s. The mussels have since clogged water intakes and mobbed native mussels, colonizing on top of them in such numbers that they are unable to move, breed or eat.

Zebra mussels are also efficient filter feeders, and in their sheer numbers have managed to clarify the waters of Lake Erie. While this effect may seem positive, the clearer water means more growth for aquatic plants, which in turn can bungle up boat motors and blemish beaches. And as it turns out, zebra mussels are picky eaters. Scientists with the Great Lakes Environmental Research Laboratory have used special camera equipment to film the mussels as they filter. What they found is that the mussels will spit out *Microcystis aeruginosa*, a type of algae that produces toxins. So not only do the mussels spare the *Microcystis* algae, but they also continue to gobble its competitors. And as a bonus, the mussels excrete phosphate and ammonia, which fertilize the growth of *Microcystis*.

These actions are part of a chain of events that help explain why Lake Erie and Saginaw Bay in Lake Huron have seen the reappearance of immense algal blooms—something Great Lakes residents had hoped was over following efforts to control phosphate emissions in the 1970s. Despite the hundreds of millions of dollars the mussels have cost businesses and taxpayers in the region and the complex problems they continue to cause, the reaction to prevent similar invasions by other bivalves has been achingly slow. Twenty years later, Canada and the U.S. are still being criticized for their weak regulations on the issue.

The State of the Great Lakes report says the presence of invasive species can be linked to many current ecosystem challenges, including the decline in the population of a small shrimp-like crustacean called *Diporeia*, which serves as food for whitefish, lake trout and smelt. The invaders are also linked to fish and waterfowl diseases, and excessive algal growth. While shipping continues to be a major concern for the introduction and spread of invasive species, the report says the roles of canals, online purchase of aquatic plants and the aquarium and fish-bait industries are receiving increasing attention.

One potential invader now at the very doorstep of the Great Lakes basin is a large Asian fish. These carp terrify commercial fishermen and recreational boaters. "Asian carp" is a generic term that describes several related species that originate in Asia. There are two species currently spreading fear in North America: bighead carp and silver carp. They are to be feared because they have the ability to spread rapidly, reproduce in large numbers and become the predominant species in an ecosystem, Michael Hansen, a professor of fisheries in Wisconsin, told a congressional committee in 2010. "Once established, fishery managers have little chance to control the fish," said Hansen, who is also chairman of the Great Lakes Fishery Commission.

In an all-too familiar story, these species were actually purposefully imported into the southern United States. It was thought they could keep aquaculture facilities clean because they are filter feeders that feast on algae and microscopic animals. The two species were brought into the country in the early 1970s from China and eastern Siberia, Hansen said. Inevitably, they escaped. By 1980, the fish were in Arkansas, Louisiana and Kentucky.

Their habit of feeding voraciously on the bottom of the food chain menu meant many native fishes were going hungry. Hansen said that a 1999 investigation of a fish kill in off-channel waters of a National Wildlife Refuge near St. Louis documented that Asian carp made up 97 percent of the biomass. There were so many that commercial fishermen were abandoning their traditional fishing sites because they were unable to lift nets loaded with Asian carp. Today, commercial fishers in the Illinois River regularly catch upward of 11,000 kilograms of bighead carp and silver carp per day, Hansen reported. Unfortunately, carp are worth much less than the native fish they replaced.

Another frightening characteristic of the silver variety is its habit of launching itself out of the water at the sound of an approaching motor. The internet is rife with videos of dozens of fish flinging themselves up to 3 metres out of the water. These fish weigh up to 9 kilograms and can seriously harm humans and their property. One biologist likened a carp blow to being hit by a bowling ball. Forget about waterskiing in carp-infested waters.

The fight to keep these scary fish out of the Great Lakes hinges on an unusual fence. An electrical barrier was set up in the manmade Chicago sanitary and ship canal—the waterway that connects the Mississippi River to Lake Michigan. The wall of electric current generated by the fence is meant to convince the fish to turn around.

Environmentalists don't think it's enough; what if the power fails? The Great Lakes' fishery involves over 1.5 million anglers and is valued at more than US$7 billion annually, according to the American Sportfishing Association. On the Canadian side of the border, the Department of Fisheries and Oceans published a risk assessment of carp in 2004 that said the fish could survive in a large swath of the country. There is much nervousness about the task facing the Americans.

Herb Gray says he thinks carp can be kept out of the Great Lakes, if there's real resolve starting at the level of the president in the U.S. and similar resolve in Canada. But he says this carp issue is one reason that there is a need to update the Great Lakes Water Quality Agreement promptly. An update is actually way overdue. "There has to be a new agreement," says Gray, adding that it has to take into account matters that weren't mentioned or barely mentioned in the existing agreement. "There's little or nothing about alien invasive species. There are lists of chemicals which are not relevant anymore and there are new chemicals not mentioned, for example, fire retardants…and so on. There are human pharmaceuticals that are turning up." He also thinks there has to be more attention paid to preserving and restoring wetlands, and dealing with issues such as runoff from hardened surfaces, municipalities and huge factory farms.

When Gray left the International Joint Commission in January 2010, he grumbled about the long delay in finishing the renegotiation process. During his tenure, there had been a major effort to address these issues, which included consultations with 4000 people around the lakes in all sorts of meetings. By 2009, "all the spade work had been done" for a new or updated agreement, but the only way to complete the work with an international agreement is to have a formal negotiation involving diplomatic representatives for Canada and the U.S.

On January 27, 2010, senior officials from Environment Canada, Foreign Affairs and International Trade Canada, the U.S. Department of State and the U.S. Environmental Protection Agency met to begin their negotiations. The two countries intend to wrap things up by the end of 2010. President Barack Obama, who hails from Chicago, has signalled serious interest in the Great Lakes by providing US$475 million for a new Environmental Protection Agency–led, interagency Great Lakes restoration initiative in his 2010 budget.

CHAPTER NINE

Clear Opportunities for the Future

WHILE THE GREAT LAKES promise to suck up a lot of funds for caretaking, cleanup and research, Ontario's premier also sees a crystal clear opportunity for citizens to make some money on the resource.

In the spring of 2010, Ontario's Liberal government introduced a Water Opportunities Act that it hopes will make the province a leader in the development and sale of new technologies and services for water conservation and treatment. When the government introduced the idea, it pointed to a 2008 Conference Board of Canada report that estimated the global market for water technology at more than US$400 billion per year—and doubling every five to six years. "In the next 20 years, worldwide demand for water is expected to be 40 percent greater than current supply—a crisis in the making if the world does not act," the government said. "Already, Ontario is beginning to provide solutions." Premier Dalton McGuinty wants the clean-water technology sector to expand on the 22,000 jobs it already holds and attract even more clean-water expertise and investment to the province, making it the clean-water capital of North America.

There is certainly a growing demand for clean-water technology. A key pressure point and opportunity will be the federal government's new regulations for municipal wastewater.

There is also growing interest in learning how efficiently different companies use water. In 2010, the same organization that pressures companies to share their carbon emissions decided to put water efficiency under the microscope, too. The Carbon Disclosure Project holds the largest database of corporate climate change information in the world. The data is gathered to aid business and policy decision making. CDP Water Disclosure will do the same for water use, helping institutional investors better understand the business risks and opportunities associated with water scarcity and other water-related issues. In 2010, CDP Water Disclosure sent a questionnaire on behalf of institutional investors to approximately 300 of the world's largest corporations in water-intensive sectors. Companies were asked to measure and disclose information on water usage, the risks and opportunities in their own operations and their supply chains, as well as water management and improvement plans. Results are expected in late 2010.

Then there is the escalating issue with nutrient pollution of lakes. Most (82 percent) Canadians are concerned with the quality of water in the lakes in which they swim, with concern being highest in Ontario (87 percent) and Quebec (87 percent), and lower in Alberta (80 percent), Saskatchewan and Manitoba (78 percent), British Columbia (72 percent) and Atlantic Canada (71 percent), according to an Ipsos Reid poll conducted in early 2010. Cracking down on the multitude of nutrient sources responsible for algal growth in lakes will require serious investment in nutrient recovery and pollution prevention technologies.

Perhaps fortuitously, this need to capture nutrients coincides with growing rumblings about "peak phosphorus." Similar to the concept of peak oil, experts are now saying we are rapidly exhausting the world's stock of mineable rock phosphate. "Within the Canadian Prairies, 'peak phosphorus' could have serious economic consequences," notes the International Institute for Sustainable Development in a December 2009 paper. "Rising fertilizer costs will hit the bottom lines of agricultural producers, which may result in higher food costs. Phosphorus mismanagement is also being exhibited within the waterbodies of the region. Lake Winnipeg, which drains the Canadian Prairies, is the most eutrophic large lake in the world. This situation clearly points to a need to better manage phosphorus resources by finding more effective ways to use, recover and recycle this precious nutrient."

The responsibility for developing a phosphorus-secure future cannot be solely imposed on agriculture, the institute says. We should all share responsibility. "This amounts to adopting a life-cycle, cradle-to-grave approach to phosphorus-based products, which include fertilizers, food and fibre." The institute recommends everything from existing technology, such as at Edmonton's waste-water treatment plant, to recovering human urine, which apparently makes an excellent fertilizer, to the 166,283 tonnes of phosphorus produced by livestock annually as a source of phosphorus.

A team of feedlot operators in Alberta has thoroughly grasped the concept. The Highmark Renewables slogan is, "Where there is waste, there is opportunity." The Kotelko and Chrapko brothers have been steadily adding to their chain of spinoff products. By 2011, the latest stage should be complete: an ethanol production plant teamed up with one of the world's largest anaerobic digestion plants, producing what they say will be the most energy efficient fuel commercially available. The ethanol plant is powered by almost 100 percent renewable energy made from a daily load of 400 tonnes of cattle manure from their feedlot. Using the manure in this way reduces the odour and nutrient-loading issues associated with stockpiling and land-applying manure and enables the company to pump out a nutrient-stabilized, odour-free, bio-based fertilizer. The other "product" that comes out of this carefully planned facility is reusable water. The operation keeps manure from contaminating nearby streams, rivers and lakes, and produces energy, fertilizer and clean water.

Conclusion

SURELY, THE HOLISTIC APPROACH taken at Highmark Renewables is the way of the future. It's widely acknowledged that if we want to continue to live within the means that nature dictates without giving serious thought to curbing population growth, then we definitely need to tighten up our wasteful ways. We won't be able to afford to waste water. And why would we want to, anyway? Using water in a more efficient way and avoiding contamination of that supply can save money while at the same time protecting human health and the environment.

But society needs to come to a common understanding that we need to move in a less wasteful direction. There are other options, of course, but they inevitably involve more conflict and the prospect of ever more people being left with less water. In Canada, it comes down to understanding how little "extra" water there is to go around, and grasping how precious water really is. Failing to do so constitutes the biggest threat to our country's water security.

Maude Barlow believes this failure stems from our childhood. "...[It's] this myth of abundance, this lesson we learned back in Grade 6 that we are blessed with so much water and anyway the amount of water in the hydrologic cycle is fixed, therefore you can't ruin it, you can't destroy it, you can use all you want and it will just go back in the cycle and come back around. And I think we're cursed with that, with that notion that there's nothing we could do to ruin our water and we could never run out. And therefore it's never a political issue in elections, or very seldom a political issue. People aren't fighting about it here in our country the way they are in other countries, you know, literally physically, violently. So we just go on our merry way thinking we have all the water in the world."

BIBLIOGRAPHY

Abell, R., et al. "Freshwater Ecoregions of the World: A New Map of Biogeographic Units for Freshwater Biodiversity Conservation." *BioScience* 58 (5): 403–414 (2008).

Allmyr, M., et. al. "Triclosan in Plasma and Milk from Swedish Nursing Mothers and Their Exposure via Personal Care Products." *Science of the Total Environment* 372 (1): 87–93 (December 2006).

American Sportfishing Association. *Sportfishing in America: An Economic Engine and Conservation Powerhouse.* 2008.

Annin, P. *The Great Lakes Water Wars.* Island Press, 2006.

Amway, M., et. al. "Epigenetic Transgenerational Actions of Endocrine Disruptors and Male Fertility." *Science* 308 (5727): 1466–1469 (June 2005).

Australia, Government of. "Australia's National Rainwater and Greywater Initiative." http://www.environment.gov.au/water/policy-programs/nrgi/index.html.

Bakker, K., edited by. *Eau Canada: The Future of Canada's Water.* UBC Press, 2007.

Botts, L. and P. Muldoon. *The Great Lakes Water Quality Agreement: Its Past Successes and Uncertain Future.* The Institute on International Environmental Governance, Dartmouth College, 1996.

Boyd, D. *Canada vs. the OECD: An Environmental Comparison.* 2001.

BP. *Statistical Review of World Energy.* June 2009.

Buckthought, M. *Tritium on Tap: Keep Radioactive Tritium Out of Our Drinking Water.* Sierra Club Canada, 2009.

Calgary, City of. *2009 Water Efficiency Report.* 2010.

Canada Mortgage and Housing Corporation. *Assessment of Ecologically Engineered Stormwater Management.* 2009.

———. *Dual-flush Toilet Project.* 2002.

———. *Energy and Water Tune-Ups for Multi-Unit Residential Buildings: A Guide for Property Owners, Managers and Custodial Staff.* 2007.

———. *Evaluation of Water-Efficient Toilet Technologies to Carry Waste in Drainlines.* 2007.

———. *Evaluating the Feasibility and Developing Design Requirements and Tools for Large-Scale Rainwater Harvesting in Ontario.* 2009.

———. *Water Reuse Standards and Verification Protocol.* 2005.

Canadian Biodiversity Web Site. http://canadianbiodiversity.mcgill.ca/english/index.htm.

Canadian Hydropower Association. *Hydropower in Canada: Past Present and Future.* 2008. http://www.canhydropower.org/hydro_e/pdf/hydropower_past_present_future_en.pdf.

Eggerston, L. "Investigative Report: 1766 Boil-Water Advisories Now in Place across Canada." *Canadian Medical Association Journal* 178 (10): 1261–1263 (May 2008).

Canadian Museum of Nature. "American Bison." *Natural History Notebooks,* 2010. http://nature.ca/notebooks/english/bison.htm.

Centers for Disease Control. *Fourth National Report on Human Exposure to Environmental Chemicals*. 2009. http://www.cdc.gov/exposurereport.

Cressy, J. "Celebrating the Beginning of the End of Bottled Water in Canada." Polaris Institute, December 2, 2009. http://www.polarisinstitute.org/celebrating_the_beginning_of_the_end_of_bottled_water_in_canada.

Ecojustice. *Flushing Out the Truth: Sewage Dumping in Ontario*. June 2009 (revised July 2009). http://www.ecojustice.ca/publications/flushing-the-truth.

Environment Canada. *2008 Municipal Water Pricing Report: Municipal Water Pricing, 2004 Statistics*. 2008. http://www.ec.gc.ca/eau-water/default. asp?lang=En&n=AE97B7F3-1.

———. *Canadian Environmental Sustainability Indicators Report*. http://www.ec.gc.ca/indicateurs-indicators/default.asp?lang=En&n=68DE8F72-1.

———. *Federal Water Policy*. 1987. http://www.ec.gc.ca/eau-water/default. asp?lang=En&n=D11549FA-1.

———. *Threats to Water Availability in Canada*. National Water Research Institute. NWRI Scientific Assessment Report Series 3 and ACSD Science Assessment Series 1, 2004.

Fair, P., et.al. "Occurrence of Triclosan in Plasma of Wild Atlantic Bottlenose Dolphins (*Tursiops truncatus*) and in Their Environment." *Environmental Pollution* 157 (8–9): 2248–2254 (August–September 2009).

Fairlie, I. *Tritium Hazard Report: Pollution and Radiation Risk from Canadian Nuclear Facilities*. Greenpeace, 2007.

Furlong, K. and K. Bakker. *Achieving Water Conservation: Strategies for Good Governance (Policy Report)*. UBC Program on Water Governance & Infrastructure Canada, 2008.

Furlong, K., C. Cook and K. Bakker. *Good Governance for Water Conservation: A Primer*. UBC Program on Water Governance & Infrastructure Canada, 2008.

Gingras, F. *Northern Waters: A Realistic, Sustainable and Profitable Plan to Exploit Quebec's Blue Gold*. Montreal Economic Institute, 2009.

Gleick, P. "Basic Water Requirements for Human Activities: Meeting Basic Needs." *Water International* 21: 83–92 (1996).

Griswold, E. "Drinking Water: Inside the Bottle." *Canadian Restaurant and Foodservice News*, October 28, 2009. http://www.foodservicenews.ca/template/beverage/archives/drinking_water_inside_the_bottle_oct_28_09.asp#ixzz0gwudJCo8.

Halford, B. "Side Effects: Pharmaceuticals Have Been Finding Their Way into Our Environment for a Long Time, but Just What Are They Doing There?" *Chemical and Engineering News* 86 (8): 13–17 (February 25, 2008).

Hayes, T., et. al. "Atrazine Induces Complete Feminization and Chemical Castration in Male African Clawed Frogs (*Xenopus laevis*)." *Proceedings of the National Academy of Sciences* 107 (10): 4612–4617 (March 2010). http://www.pnas.org/content/107/10/4612.full.

Health Canada. *Drinking Water Advisories in First Nations Communities in Canada: A National Overview 1995–2007*. 2009.

Heinmiller, T. "Path Dependency and Collective Action in Common Pool Governance." *International Journal of the Commons* 3 (1): 131–147 (2009).

Hrudey, S. and E. Hrudey. *Safe Drinking Water: Lessons from Recent Outbreaks in Affluent Nations*. IWA Publishing, 2004.

Hutchings, J. and M. Festa-Bianchet. "Canadian Species at Risk (2006–2008), with Particular Emphasis on Fishes." *Environmental Reviews* 17: 53–65 (2009).

Hydro-Quebec. *2009 Comparison of Electricity Prices in Major North American Cities*. 2009. http://www.hydroquebec.com/publications/en/comparison_ prices/pdf/comp_2009_en.pdf.

International Joint Commission. *Advice to Governments on Their Review of the Great Lakes Water Quality Agreement: A Special Report to the Governments of Canada and the United States*. 2006.

———. *Great Lakes Diversions and Consumptive Uses: A Report to the Governments of the United States and Canada*. 1985.

———. *Protection of the Waters of the Great Lakes: Final Report to the Governments of Canada and the United States*. 2000.

Kahn, P., Jr. "Children's Affiliations with Nature: Structure, Development and the Problem of Environmental Generational Amnesia." In *Children and Nature: Psychological, Sociocultural and Evolutionary Investigations*, edited by P.H. Kahn, Jr. and S.R. Kellert. MIT Press, 2002.

Kidd, K., et. al. "Collapse of a Fish Population After Exposure to a Synthetic Estrogen." *Proceedings of the National Academy of Sciences* 104 (21): 8897–8901 (May 22, 2007).

Lake Winnipeg Research Consortium Inc. *Report on Science, Education and Outreach Activities, April 1, 2008–March 31, 2009*. 2009.

Lake Winnipeg Stewardship Board. *Reducing Nutrient Loading to Lake Winnipeg and its Watershed: Our Collective Responsibility and Commitment to Action*. December 2006.

Lynch-Stewart Associates. *Wetlands of International Importance (RAMSAR Sites) in Canada: Survey of RAMSAR Site Managers 2007 Final Report*. March 2008.

Mandrak, N. and B. Cudmore. *Risk Assessment for Asian Carps in Canada*. Fisheries and Oceans Canada, 2004.

Milko, R. "Potential Ecological Effects of the Proposed GRAND Canal Diversion Project on Hudson and James Bays." *Arctic* 39 (4): 316–326 (December 1986).

Montana and Alberta Joint Initiative Team. *St. Mary and Milk River Water Management Initiative Joint Status Report #11*. January 25, 2010.

Morin, A. and B. Cantin. *Strengthening Integrated Water Resource Management in Canada: Discussion Paper*. Policy Research Initiative, 2009.

National Defence. "Presence of TCE in Groundwater at Valcartier Garrison." January 30, 2004, updated January 29, 2010. http://www.forces.gc.ca/site/news-nouvelles/ news-nouvelles-eng.asp?cat=00&cat=00&id=3265.

Northwest Territories, Government of. *Northern Voices, Northern Waters: NWT Water Stewardship Strategy*. May 2010.

Ontario Drinking Water Advisory Council. *Report and Advice on the Ontario Drinking Water Quality Standard for Tritium*. 2009.

Ontario Ministry of the Environment. *Survey of the Occurrence of Pharmaceuticals and Other Emerging Contaminants in Untreated Source and Finished Drinking Water in Ontario*. 2010.

Ottawa, City of. "Tritium Levels in Ottawa Drinking Water." Memo to Mayor and Members of Council from General Manager, Environmental Services Department, November 19, 2009. http://www.ottawa.ca/residents/water/tritium_nov09_en.html.

Phare, M.S. *Review of the Final Report of Expert Panel on First Nations' Drinking Water to the Assembly of First Nations*. Centre for Indigenous Environmental Resources, Inc., 2006.

Pinto, U. and B. Maheshwari. "Reuse of Greywater for Irrigation around Homes in Australia: Understanding Community Views, Issues and Practices." *Urban Water Journal*, 7 (2): 141–153 (April 2010).

Polaris Institute, Assembly of First Nations and the Canadian Labour Congress. *Boiling Point: Six Community Profiles of the Water Crisis Facing First Nations within Canada*. 2008.

Policy Research Initiative. *Does Pricing Water Reduce Agricultural Demand? An Example from British Columbia*. 2007.

Pomeroy, J., D. de Boer and L.W. Martz. *Hydrology and Water Resources of Saskatchewan, Centre for Hydrology Report #1*. Centre for Hydrology, University of Saskatchewan, 2005.

Pope, A. *Report on the Kashechewan First Nation and Its People*. 2006.

Prowse, T., F. Wrona and G. Power. Threats to Water Availability in Canada. Environment Canada, National Water Research Institute, 2004.

Public Health Agency of Canada. *C-EnterNet Short Report*. 2008.

———. *Laboratory Surveillance Data for Enteric Pathogens in Canada: Annual Summary*. 2006.

Quebec, Government of. *An Act to Affirm the Collective Nature of Water Resources and Provide for Increased Water Resource Protection*. 2009. http://www.canlii.org/en/qc/laws/stat/rsq-c-c-6.2/latest/rsq-c-c-6.2.html.

———. Water Resources Preservation Act. 2001.

Quinn, F. *Water Diversion, Export and Canada–US Relations: A Brief History*. Program on Water Issues, Munk Centre for International Studies, 2007.

Reisner, M. *Cadillac Desert: The American West and its Disappearing Water*. Penguin Books, 1993.

Sauchyn, D. and S. Kulshreshtha. "Chapter 7: Prairies." In *From Impacts to Adaptation: Canada in a Changing Climate 2007*, edited by D.S. Lemmem, et al. Government of Canada, 2008.

Schindler, D. and J. Vallentyne. *The Algal Bowl: Overfertilization of the World's Freshwater and Estuaries*. University of Alberta Press, 2008.

Schneider, M. *Sales of 13L Toilets versus Low-Flush Models in Canada (2005)*. The Canadian Water and Wastewater Association, June 2007.

Smol, J. and M. Douglas. "Crossing the Final Ecological Threshold in High Arctic Ponds." *Proceedings of the National Academy of Sciences* 104 (30): 12395–12397 (July 24, 2007).

Soulard, F. *Watering Accounting at Statistics Canada: The Inland Fresh Water Assets Account.* London Group of Environmental Accounting, 2003.

Statistics Canada. *Households and the Environment 2007.* Environment Accounts and Statistics Division, System of National Accounts, 2009.

———. *Human Activity and the Environment: Freshwater Supply and Demand in Canada.* 2010.

———. *Human Activity and the Environment: Annual Statistics.* 2009.

———. *Human Activity and the Environment: Climate Change in Canada.* 2008.

Swain, H., S. Hrudey and S. Louttit. *Report of the Expert Panel on Safe Drinking Water for First Nations.* November 2006.

Sweeney, R. "Rejuvenation of Lake Erie." *GeoJournal* 35 (1): 65–66 (1995).

Trottier, C., et al. *Murky Waters: The Urgent Need for Health and Environmental Regulations of the Bottled Water Industry.* Polaris Institute, March 25, 2009.

Ulrich, A., D. Malley and V. Voora. *Peak Phosphorus: Opportunity in the Making.* International Institute for Sustainable Development, December 2009.

United Nations Environment Programme. *Climate Change Science Compendium.* 2009.

———. *Hydropolitical Vulnerability and Resilience along International Waters: North America.* 2009.

Vanderploeg, H. *The Zebra Mussel Connection: Nuisance Algal Blooms, Lake Erie Anoxia and Other Water Quality Problems in the Great Lakes.* Great Lakes Environmental Research Laboratory, 2002.

Veldhoen, N., et al. "The Bactericidal Agent Triclosan Modulates Thyroid Hormone-Associated Gene Expression and Disrupts Postembryonic Anuran Development." *Aquatic Toxicology* 80 (3): 217–227 (December 1, 2006).

Zuccato, E., et al. "Cocaine in Surface Waters: A New Evidence-based Tool to Monitor Community Drug Abuse." *Environmental Health* 4 (14): 2005.

Index

Credits

p. 15. "Distribution of Earth's Water." Credit: U.S. Geological Survey, public domain.

p. 16. "How Much of Earth's Water is Available for Our Use." Credit: U.S. Geological Survey, public domain.

p. 21. "The Largest Canadian Lakes and the Volume of Water They Hold." Data gathered by author from numerous sources.

p. 22. "Longest Rivers in Canada." Reproduced with the permission of Natural Resources Canada 2010, courtesy of the Atlas of Canada.

p. 23. "Maximum Discharge of Rivers in Canada." Reproduced with the permission of Natural Resources Canada 2010, courtesy of the Atlas of Canada.

p. 25. Source: "Ocean Drainage Areas and Drainage Regions of Canada." Adapted from Statistics Canada, *Currents of Change: Final Report of the Inquiry on Federal Water Policy*, Environment Canada, Ottawa. Released 2009.

p. 33. Source: "definition of point source and non-point source pollution." Ontario Ministry of the Environment.

p. 34. Source: National Pollutant Release Inventory NPRI) 2008 Facility Data Summary, http://www.ec.gc.calinrp-npri/default.asp?lang=En&m:CFA83D44-l, Environment Canada, 2009. Reproduced with the permission of the Minister of Public Works and Government Services Canada, [2010].

p. 45. "Lake Winnipeg Watershed" map. Credit: Lyle Lockhart, Lake Winnipeg Foundation. Used by permission.

p. 80. Source: "statement on half-life of tritium." Canadian Nuclear Safety Commission.

p. 113. "Mackenzie Drainage Basin" map. Adapted with the permission of Natural Resources Canada 2010, courtesy of the Atlas of Canada.

p. 119. Source: "Freshwater Fish That Have Gone Extinct." Committee on the Status of Endangered Wildlife in Canada (COSEWIC).

p. 121. "Paddlefish." Credit: Timothy Knepp / U.S. Fish and Wildlife Service, public domain.

p. 134. "Great Lakes Diversions." Credit: derived from U.S. Army Corps of Engineers, Detroit District publication "Anthropogenic Changes to Great Lakes Water Levels", 1999.

p. 135. "James Bay Project—Rupert River Diversion". Credit: adapted from "Rupert River Diversion map," Brian Back / Ottertooth.com. Used by permission.

p. 139. Source: "International Joint Commission's work summarized." Environment Canada.

p. 140. Source: "Canada - United States Transboundary Basins," http://www.ec.gc.ca/eau-water/default.asp?lang=En&n=B947BAA8-1, Environment Canada, 2010. Reproduced with the permission of the Minister of Public Works and Government Services, 2010.

p. 142. "Old Man River Basin and Milk River Basin," map from "Activities in Transboundary Drainage Basins.pdf" found at http://www.ijc.org/rel/pdf/map-activities-in-transboundary-drainage-basins.pdf. Used by permission of International Joint Commission, 2010.

p. 143. "Columbia River Basin," map from "Activities in Transboundary Drainage Basins.pdf" found at http://www.ijc.org/rel/pdf/map-activities-in-transboundary-drainage-basins.pdf. Used by permission of International Joint Commission, 2010.

p. 151. "Satellite Photos of the Aral Sea in 1989 and 2008." File is in public domain because it was created by NASA. Retrieved from http://en.wikipedia.org/wiki/File:Aral_Sea_1989-2008.jpg

p. 164. "Major Water Uses in Canada (Industrial, Municipal and Agricultural)." Graph based on author's text (author's data gathered from Statistics Canada and Environment Canada information).

p. 165. Source: "How many litres of water does it take to produce." Hoekstra and Chapagain, Environment Canada.

p. 169. "How Water is Consumed in the Home." Graph based on author's text.

HANNEKE BROOYMANS began her journalism career in science labs at the University of Alberta. It was a place not overly populated with writers at the time. After earning a Bachelor of Science degree in environmental biology, the notion of communicating all those lessons dawned on her one day. Hanneke is now an experienced journalist who has served as an environment reporter at the *Edmonton Journal* for the past nine years. During that time, she has been a member of the Society of Environmental Journalists. As a journalist, she feels her duty is always to provide citizens with the most thorough, relevant and up-to-date information possible so they can make up their own minds about what needs to be done about environmental issues. After that, it's up to them.